Table of Contents

Unsolved 2001

- John Marzetti
- Tony Lawlor
- John Hall and David McIntosh
- Dean Eccleston
- Patrick Erhabor
- Geoff Gray
- Ian Clarke
- Lindsey Chezine Scholes
- Yasser Nazir
- Naziat Parveen Zafar
- Carlton McDonald
- Frederick Baker
- Patrick Pasipanodya
- Martin Silvester
- Michael James Cabey
- Phillip Saville
- Jimmy Millen
- Makram Abdul-Kadir
- Andrew Chubb
- Daniel Dale
- Richie Clayton
- Cherie Melgram
- Hugh Scott
- Oguzhin Ozdemir
- Julie Foster
- Mithat Lleshi
- Ouahid Chakib
- John Holland
- Mohammed Warsame
- Alec Christopher
- Jody Burns
- Colin Beer

- John Dickinson
- Christopher Hewitt
- Jacey Frederick Valentine John Charles
- Donovan Williams
- Sami Mustafa and Hasan Mamali
- Richard Rayner
- Billy Webb
- Mary Hancock
- Andre Jan Aylward
- Steven Daniel Richard McCalla
- Hilda Lockert
- Corey Wright and Wayne Henry
- Rebecca Hall
- David George Roads
- Mehmet Selimoglu
- Florence Ansell
- Mark Thompson and George Price
- Corey Brown
- Stuart Lubbock
- Herbert Schwarz
- David Williamson
- Ian Michael Dowling
- Baby
- John Swain
- Peter Beaumont Gowling
- Mark Connor
- Francis Cross
- Hussain Obad
- Akbal Brar
- Frank Anthony Holmes
- Andrew Michael Williams
- Isa-Din Shire

- Anthony Boyle

Unsolved 2001

A list of unsolved cases for 2001.

Michael French

Age: unknown

Sex: male

Date: 31 Dec 2001

Place: Oatlands Estate, Clapham

Michael French was stabbed at a party.

A man was tried for his murder but acquitted.

Michael French had been at a party on New Year's Eve when two men burst into the flat and accused Michael French of stealing some money. One of the men was then seen to lunge towards Michael French and punch at him twice but it was found that the man had had a knife wrapped up in a cloth of some description and he had stabbed Michael French twice.

It was said that the other people at the party had been taking drugs.

He was taken to King's College Hospital by air ambulance where an operation was carried out but he died at 8am. The stab wounds had penetrated his chest and damaged a large artery and he had died from internal bleeding.

A man was charged with his murder but he said that he had left the party earlier to go to Tulse Hill to buy some crack cocaine. He said that he had been at the party earlier and had been outside at one point smoking a spliff but said that he went off to buy drugs and Michael French had gone back into the party.

Donald Marlow Harriot

Age: 28

Sex: male

Date: 30 Dec 2001

Place: Clapton, East London

Donald Marlow Harriot was beaten to death at his home.

His death was published as unresolved by the Metropolitan Police in a Freedom of Information Request but no further information is known.

Douglas McPherson

Age: 42

Sex: male

Date: 26 Dec 2001

Place: London Tavern, Hackney

Douglas McPherson was killed in the London Tavern in Hackney on Boxing Day.

A man was tried for his murder but acquitted. It was noted that he was not charged with having actually inflicting the blows that killed Douglas McPherson, but rather on the basis of joint enterprise.

Douglas McPherson died after four men burst into a pub and attacked him and another man. He was hit over the head with a baseball bat and taken to hospital where he later died. The other man survived.

It was said that there were fifteen regular drinkers in the London Tavern at the time who all fled to the toilets when the four men came into the pub and only one witness was said to have provided evidence saying that the man tried was one of the attackers. At the trial a barrister noted that the eye witness evidence was inconsistent.

The man that was tried for his murder had earlier been thrown out of the London Tavern for hogging the punch bowl. Whilst outside he had also had an argument with his ex-girlfriend and her family and had then gone home. However, his mother said that after he got home she had to wrestle him down to stop him going back to the pub saying that he was furious that his ex-girlfriend and her family had sided with the landlord over him being thrown out and that he had wanted to go back and finish the argument with them. His mother said that she knew judo and that her son was paralytic at the time. She said that she had sat on him for a good couple of hours until he calmed down and went to sleep.

The man later blamed his brother who had since vanished. However, it was noted that he had not blamed him until 10-months after he had been arrested.

It was also heard that the man who was tried's brother was alleged to have said that he had been involved with the attack and that he had admitted smashing the punch bowl to pieces.

After the trial the police refused to comment on whether they would continue the murder investigation to look for the man's brother.

Mr Long

Age: 40

Sex: male

Date: 19 Dec 2001

Place: Gloucester, Gloucestershire

Mr Long died at his home in Gloucester.

He was black and the pathologist that carried out his post-mortem said that he could not say whether his injuries had resulted from an assault or an accident.

His death was reported in a Gloucestershire Police Freedom of Information request and no other details are known.

Glenda Chambers

Age: 70

Sex: female

Date: 14 Dec 2001

Place: Onley Road, Walworth, London

Glenda Chambers died in a fire at her home.

A 33-year-old man was tried for her murder but acquitted.

Glenda Chambers suffered from burns and smoke inhalation and died a week later in hospital. She had lived in a maisonette.

One of Glenda Chambers's daughters was found outside after having jumped from a balcony and another relative, a nephew managed to escape.

It was said that the man, who had been in a relationship with two of Glenda Chambers's daughters over a four-year period, had started the fire after a row over him cheating with the daughters came to a head.

However, the man, who was a taxi-driver, said that at the time he had been driving along the M1 near Bedford saying that he had had a fare from London to go to a village in Bedford but said that he couldn't remember the name of the village. He said that he had never been out of London before and didn't know how far the destination was. The court also heard that the evidence against him was all circumstantial and that there were no witnesses or any scientific evidence.

Glenda Chambers and the man had met five years earlier. The man and Glenda Chambers's 23-year-old daughter were both church goers. The 23-year-old daughter had wanted to get married but the man didn't want to. However, later, the man began seeing Glenda Chambers's younger 19-year-old daughter who then moved in with him and had his child. However, after five months they split up and the man later fell out with the whole family.

The court heard that Glenda Chambers didn't like the fact that the man was seeing both of her daughters.

The day after the fire the man returned to his native Uganda. However, he returned a month later and was arrested at Heathrow Airport.

Wayne Julian

Age: 20

Sex: male

Date: 14 Dec 2001

Place: Hackney Road, London

Wayne Julian was shot in Hackney Road.

He was unemployed.

Nothing more is known.

Charlotte Latta

Age: 10 weeks

Sex: female

Date: 4 Dec 2001

Place: Byron Close, Bishops Waltham, Hampshire

Charlotte Latta died from multiple injuries.

Her father was tried for her murder but acquitted.

She had brain damage and 33 bone fractures to her arms, legs and ribs.

In court, it was said that she had been assaulted on various dates. She was taken to the Royal Hampshire County Hospital in Winchester on 2 December 2001 after she went limp whilst her father was feeding her, and her injuries were discovered. She was put on a life support machine but it was switched off on 4 December 2001.

Charlotte Latta had been seen with her father leaving a hospital earlier in the day on 2 December 2001 after Charlotte Latta had a routine check-up where she was described as being bright and alert. She had had problems with her feeding previously and had been in hospital for a number of days the month before.

Her father said that he had been feeding her at home and 'Almost instantly her eyes started to shut, I remember thinking 'she cannot go to sleep', so I took the bottle out of her mouth and she started to make a deep wheezing sound and I saw her eyeballs roll back into her head and she started to go limp.'. He then took her to the hospital.

The prosecution said that he had violently shaken her whilst he was feeding her in an upstairs room whilst the rest of his family were downstairs having a meal.

It was also said that as well as being shaken, her head had been hit against a solid surface.

Her father was acquitted after it was heard that it could not be proved that he had been responsible or that he had deliberately harmed her.

However, the judge said, 'That someone had abused Charlotte Latta is beyond doubt. While her father is one of those who could have inflicted those injuries, there is absolutely no evidence that he did so.'.

The police said 'It is clear that Charlotte received inflicted injuries over a period of time prior to her death. Exhaustive inquiries were completed after Charlotte's death to try and establish who was responsible. The police do not intend to reopen this investigation.'.

Rajnikant Pandya

Age: 37

Sex: male

Date: 28 Nov 2001

Place: Anitas Off-licence, Sutton Common Road, Sutton

Rajnikant Pandya was shot in Anita's Off-licence in Watford during a robbery.

He ran the off-licence.

He was shot twice in the stomach and the heart and died almost instantly.

CCTV evidence was captured of the shooting which showed a man wearing an animal mask and dressed in dark clothing come in and shoot him at around 9.10pm.

It was noted that the murderer had fled without taking any money and that £140 was left behind in the till.

Soon after the shooting some boys were seen to run across the street. The police said that they didn't know if they were involved but wanted to speak to them to rule them out of their investigations.

At the time he was shot his two daughters, aged 9 and 16, had been upstairs in their home above the shop where they all lived.

Anita's Off-licence was on the corner of Sutton Common Road and Ridge Road.

Rajnikant Pandya's brother said that Rajnikant Pandya had been scared of crime and as such had been planning to move back to India.

Brian Hardwick

Age: 50

Sex: male

Date: 21 Nov 2001

Place: Huddersfield Car Electricals, Colne Road

Brian Hardwick was shot dead at his workplace, Huddersfield Car Electricals on Colne Road.

He had been shot twice, once in the chest and once in the back of the head. He was last seen alive at 5.30pm on 21 November 2001 his body was found the following morning at 8pm.

When he was first found the police thought that his death was due to natural causes, however, when they saw a head injury they ordered a post-mortem to be carried out during which it was said that a Home Office pathologist was shocked to find that he had gun shot injuries.

The pathologist that carried out his post-mortem said that his shooting amounted to an execution. He said that he thought that Brian Hardwick had been fixing his puncture at the time as when he was found he still had the dust cap in his hand.

It was said that a man had deliberately punctured Brian Hardwick's car tyre so that Brian Hardwick would stay on at the garage after his colleagues went home.

After he was shot his wallet was stolen and minutes later £350 was withdrawn from his account at a cash machine at an Asda store in Fartown, Huddersfield. His purse and a chain and pendant were also found missing. He had written the PIN number for his bank card on a piece of paper in his wallet.

It had been raining on the evening he was shot.

The police said that robbery was an obvious motive but said that they thought the reason for his murder lay in his background, suggesting the possibility of a secret that he had kept from his wife. However, the police said that they could find nothing in his background that stood out as a motive for his murder.

The police said that there were four people that they were trying to identify:

The first man was white, age 35 to 45 with short dark neat hair and had been well dressed. He had turned up at the garage without an appointment a few hours earlier and had asked Brian Hardwick to look at an electrical fault in a red car but had then sworn at Brian Hardwick and stormed off.

The second man was described as being aged between 25 to 30, about 5ft 6in tall with short dark hair and wearing a dark padded jacket. He was said to have been seen staring at the garage at about 10.30am from the opposite side of Colne Road.

The third man was seen just after 4pm and was described as African-Caribbean, between 20 to 25 years of age, well built, about 5ft 5ins tall and wearing dark clothes. He was seen crouching near a window at the garage.

The fourth person was seen about 20 minutes before Brian Hardwick found the puncture on his car. he was described as white, aged 20 to 35 years old, about 5ft 9ins tall and having a stocky build and a chubby face. He was said to have had stubble, short dark hair and to have had piercing dark brown eyes and dark eyebrows. He had been wearing a dark three-quarter-length jacket with dark trousers and was seen in the car park behind the Amsterdam Bar getting into a sporty old Mini car with wide wheels. There was a young woman in the car who was said to have been aged between 18 and 25 years old and had long bleached blonde hair.

He had been married for six months and was interested in the Wild West and Country and Western music.

Horace Pinnock

Age: 29

Sex: male

Date: 20 Nov 2001

Place: Plaza Hotel, Wembley

Horace Pinnock was shot after being robbed outside the Plaza Hotel in Wembley.

He was a DJ known as DJ Village.

He was shot about 2 hours after he and some friends had been robbed of jewellery and money.

Horace Pinnock had been with some friends, three men and two women and was parking his blue Ford Galaxy car in the car park of the Plaza Hotel in Wembley at about midnight when two armed men robbed them. The armed men took money and jewellery from them. The amount of money stolen was said to have been more than £10,000 equivalent in US dollars. Most of the money had belonged to a Jamaican recording artist who had been on tour in Britain at the time and had been staying at the Plaza Hotel. They had just come back from performing live at the Ocean venue in east London.

After being robbed Horace Pinnock reported the theft to the hotel staff and the police were told.

However, soon after, at about 2am Horace Pinnock, and two of his friends were in the hotel lobby when between six and ten men came in and there was an altercation which then went out into the street where Horace Pinnock was shot.

He was taken to the Central Middlesex Hospital but pronounced dead.

Horace Pinnock had presented shows on the BBC's Radio 1 channel and it was noted that the radio station had become more and more associated with violence due to their move towards embracing more street and rap music. As well as the murder of Horace Pinnock, another DJ that had presented on Radio 1 had been shot in his car in 1999 although he was only shot in the arm and survived, whilst another DJ that had presented shows on Radio 1 admitted that he had served seventeen months in prison for drug dealing.

Horace Pinnock had hosted the Radio 1 show called Dancehall Reggae and was described as a rising star.

Brian Perry

Age: 63

Sex: male

Date: 16 Nov 2001

Place: The Blue Anchor, Bermondsey, South London

Brian Perry was shot three times outside his minicab firm, Blue Anchor, in south London.

He had just got back to his office after doing some shopping when two men in a car wearing balaclava's and dressed in black pulled up and shot him. The car had been fitted with false number plates.

He had previously been involved with laundering money from the 1983 Brinks Mat gold bullion robbery and was convicted in 1992 of handling stolen goods from the robbery and sentenced to nine years. The Brinks Mat robbery had taken place on 26 November 1983 at a warehouse at Heathrow during which £26,000,000 worth of gold was stolen and has never been recovered. The robbery had been carried out by six men who had taken 6,800 gold ingots weighing three tons.

In 2006, two men were tried for his murder but acquitted.

He was shot in the head, chest and back. It was said that he had been shot by a professional hit-man and that the motive might or might not have been connected to the Brinks Mat gold bullion robbery.

During their investigation into the two men that were tried for his murder the police searched an area where one of the men accused had earlier been seen. They used a German shepherd dog to search for evidence and found a revolver which was said to have been the gun used to shoot Brian Perry. It was said that the dog had first found the balaclava in a bin but had then put its whole head in and pulled out the revolver which was inside a sock. DNA from both of the men on trial was found on the balaclava. It was said that some of the bullets found with the gun were of the same type used in Brian Perry's murder.

One of the men had admitted owning and possessing a similar firearm to the one found but said that he had not been in the car.

The two men were acquitted of murder after it was said that there was no forensic evidence linking them to the murder and that the evidence presented was circumstantial.

Although the gold from the robbery was never recovered, two men were convicted for the robbery and sentenced to 25 years and it was said that Brian Perry was supposed to be taking care of their outside interests and had their shares of the gold but had been taking money for himself.

Brian Perry had lived in Brasted, Kent. His murder is said to be one of many unsolved and unexplained deaths associated with the Brinks Mat robbery thought to be about twenty.

Sellathurai Balasingham

Age: 36

Sex: male

Date: 7 Nov 2001

Place: Kent Close, Pollards Hill Estate, Harrow

Sellathurai Balasingham was on his way home from work when he was attacked around 11pm in a grassy area in between Kent Close and Huntington Close on the Pollards Hill Estate. Several people were convicted of his killing but later had their convictions quashed.

Sellathurai Balasingham was a Tamil and it was thought that he had been murdered by other Tamils.

He had driven into Huntingdon Close in his P-reg Honda Civic car at about 11pm on 6 November 2001 after returning home from work from the Sunlight Laundry in Deer Park Road, Wimbledon.

It was said that he was then dragged from his car, chased and kicked. He had a fractured skull, with serious injuries to his head and brain and also had a fractured shoulder blade, five broken ribs, bruising and defensive injuries.

Neighbours said that they saw Sellathurai Balasingham outside on a grassy area between Kent Close and Huntington Close on the Pollards Hill Estate being attacked and two teenagers said that they saw Sellathurai Balasingham being hit with a cricket bat.

After being attacked he was taken to the Mayday Hospital in Croydon were he was pronounced dead just after midnight on 7 November 2001. His post-mortem concluded that he had died from head injuries.

It was said that the men that were tried for his murder had attacked him because he had embarrassed a relative who also worked at the Sunlight Laundry. They were said to have followed him home from work in separate vehicles and used mobile phones to communicate with each other so as to block his escape routes. It was said that he was then dragged from his car, chased and when caught, beaten with the cricket bat.

The trial heard that one man had orchestrated the attack because of the insult at the laundry. It was heard that the attack was witnessed by several people, but none of the witnesses were able to identify the attackers although they had identified a Suzuki Swift vehicle that had been used which was later found burned out on 7 November 2001 in Kingston-on-Thames and which belonged to one of the men convicted and contained his fingerprints. It was said that the owner of the Suzuki Swift vehicle had driven three of the men to the scene. It was said that he had planned to plead guilty to conspiracy to assault at the trial and gave evidence for the prosecution which was backed up by mobile phone evidence that placed the other defendants in roughly the locations that he described.

As such, the owner of the Suzuki Swift vehicle was given bail and although not put on a witness protection scheme the police did help him to find accommodation away from the area where he had lived and he was given stringent curfew conditions. However, it later became apparent that he was not observing them and was going off to see his girlfriend and another friend and that at the trial it was found that he had vanished. However, the prosecution still put his written statement before the jury in the understanding that he had vanished and that all efforts had been made to find him.

In court, it was also noted that it could not be ruled out that he had been kept away from the court by or on behalf of the other men charged and the trial was allowed to go ahead. It was also noted that evidence was found in notes from his time on remand that he was going to present an alibi in the court and that on the basis that he had made previously inconsistent statements his evidence should be approached on that basis.

However, later, during the trial the court received a fax thought to be from the Suzuki Swift vehicle owner on 21 June 2004 from Chennai in India which read, 'I was supposed to attend the courts on 19th April 2004. But the statement that I gave was false. I was advised by the police to give a false statement. I left the country safely and now living in India. I don't want to be involved in this case anymore. I apologise for any inconvenience caused.'. However, it was later concluded that the fax was fake and was not from the Suzuki Swift vehicle owner and that it was from someone else trying to derail the trial.

The trial then went on and six men were initially convicted in relation to the murder on 19 July 2004, Four people for murder and another two for conspiracy to assault.

Then, shortly after the trial, the Suzuki Swift vehicle owner surrendered to the police and made a statement that read, 'In September 2003 I pleaded guilty to the offence of conspiracy to cause actual bodily harm. I was granted conditional bail from the Central Criminal Court and was awaiting sentence. I also was a prosecution witness and provided a witness statement implicating my co-defendants who were due to stand trial in relation to an allegation of murder. It had been my intention to attend court and provide evidence for the prosecution. Prior to the start of the trial, I was contacted by a number of Tamil males. I do not wish to name the males concerned. The males threatened me and told me that if I attended court to give evidence, I would be killed, together with members of my family. I genuinely believed these people would carry out their threats. It is for this reason I breached my bail, and I went into hiding. I do not wish to state where I went. I have been asked about a letter dated 21 June 2004 that was faxed to the Central Criminal Court from India. I have seen a copy of this letter. I have never seen this letter prior to today. I did not write this letter. Prior to today I had no knowledge this letter existed. I certainly did not sign the letter. I do not wish to say any more at this stage because I feel that if I do I may say things that put my life in danger.'.

He was then convicted and sentenced to fourteen months' imprisonment.

However, the Suzuki Swift vehicle owner was later questioned repeatedly by the police to determine where he had been during the time he had breached his bail conditions and it was found that he gave them explanations that were unsatisfactory and full of contradictions and implausibility's and as a consequence the police submitted that there was doubt over the correctness of the judge's conclusion that the Suzuki Swift vehicle owner had failed to attend the trial because of things said or done by or on behalf of the other men charged.

Further it was then found that the Suzuki Swift vehicle owner's solicitor was thoroughly dishonest and had been convicted of conspiracy to pervert the course of justice, to contempt of court, and to an offence of conspiracy to obtain money transfers by deception and of falsifying a letter to the Inland Revenue. It was also further found that the solicitor had in another case advised a witness to give evidence to support a client, regardless of what the truth might have been, and that he had also advised the person that if they were pressurised by the police that the person should go somewhere they couldn't be found.

It was also later shown that the Suzuki Swift vehicle owner had been offered £5,000 by his girlfriend not to give evidence.

As such, the men that were convicted of Sellathurai Balasingham's murder were allowed their appeal and their convictions were overturned by the Court of Appeals in 2007.

However, at a retrial in July 2008 six men were convicted for charges related to his murder, two people being convicted for his murder, two for his manslaughter and another two for conspiracy to assault.

However, on 12 April 2011 all of their convictions were quashed by the Court of Appeals due to new eyewitness evidence.

As such, the murder of Sellathurai Balasingham remains unsolved.

Abdul Mahroof

Age: 58

Sex: male

Date: 7 Nov 2001

Place: Crispian Close, Neasden

Abdul Mahroof was found hanging from his second-floor window in 1994 and was left paralysed. He died 8 years later from aspiration due to pneumonia on 7 November 2001.

Abdul Mahroof was found hanging from the second-floor window of his flat. A neighbour and emergency services loosened the knot in the rope and he was lowered to the ground. When he was lowered he was found to have a cigarette clamped in his mouth which had to be pried out before resuscitation could be carried out.

He was taken to hospital where he was declared a tetraplegic and could only move his eyes. Six months later he was moved to Walm Lane Nursing Home in Willesden where he remained for 8 years when he died of aspiration due to pneumonia.

Abdul Mahroof had lived with a lodger who was seen running off from the flat and was never seen again. It was also noted that £9,000 was missing from his flat.

Shortly before he was found hanging, a man called his daughter and told her that she would never see her father again. She said that she didn't recognise the voice but said that it wasn't her father's. She said that she then called her mother and they both rushed round to Abdul Mahroof's flat where they found him hanging.

At his inquest, the Coroner criticised the police for not investigating the matter at the time or launching a murder inquiry noting that the only information he had from the police about Abdul Mahroof's death was from the notes of a policewoman that had been called out to the scene. The Coroner noted that millions of pounds had been spent investigating the murder of Stephen Lawrence but in the case of Abdul Mahroof where his daughter had received a call a few hours before he was found hanging, where £9,000 had gone missing and where a lodger was seen running from the scene never to be seen again, all the police could present to the inquest were the notes from the policewoman's pocket book.

The lodger was not identified and was never heard from again.

Michaela Hague

Age: 25

Sex: female

Date: 5 Nov 2001

Place: Bower Street, Spitalfields, Sheffield

Michaela Hague was stabbed during an attack in Sheffield.

She was a prostitute and had been working the streets around Bower Street in Sheffield. She was picked up around 7pm and then stabbed 19 times in the neck and back and when she was next seen at about 8pm in a mostly unlit car park on some waste ground off Spitalfields she was lying in a pool of blood.

An old style blue Ford Sierra was seen driving away.

She was found semi-conscious shortly after 8pm and the police were called.

When Michaela Hague was found by a policeman she managed to describe the man that had attacked her. She told them that the man had been white, about 6ft tall, 38 years of age, was clean shaven, wearing a blue fleece jacket and had had glasses on and had a wedding ring on his finger.

She was taken to the Northern General Hospital, arriving at about 8.30pm, and later died there at 11.05pm.

However, later, at her inquest, it was heard that although she had been stabbed 19 times, she might have survived if she had undergone immediate surgery. It was said that none of the stab wounds where more than 30mm deep and that only six had punctured her lungs and the rest had missed vital organs such as her heart, aorta artery or liver. It was said that she had been at the hospital for several hours during which time there had been plenty of time for her to have undergone emergency surgery. The pathologist that carried out her post-mortem said that he had seen people with much larger vascular structures damage who had survived with surgery.

However, he added that there was no argument that the stab wounds were not 100% the cause of her death.

After her murder, a woman came forward to say that she had been in Spring Street in her Citroen car at around 9pm when she had taken a wrong turn on her way to a friend's place, and said that a strange man, who it was suggested might have been Michaela Hague's killer, stood in front of her car and wouldn't let her drive off. She said that whenever she moved her car about he moved to stand in front of it. She said that she thought that he wanted her to wind her window down and said that a few minutes later she managed to get away.

The police said that they did manage to get some DNA evidence but had not been able to identify whose it was.

It was said Michaela Hague was a heroin addict and had turned to prostitution to earn money to buy more drugs. It was said that she had been working the streets for about six months. The area that she had been working in, around Corporation Street, was a well-known red-light district.

Michaela Hague had lived on Lopham Street in Pitsmoor, Sheffield, and had a partner and a son.

Lee Foord

Age: 1

Sex: male

Date: 2 Nov 2001

Place: London

The death of Lee Foord was declared undetected by the Metropolitan Police in a Freedom of Information request.

No further information is known.

Eva Blackburn

Age: 75

Sex: female

Date: 1 Nov 2001

Place: Airedale General Hospital, Keighley

June Driver, Eva Blackburn and Annie Midgley died in hospital and were thought to have been poisoned.

A nurse was charged with their murders but she accidentally overdosed on anti-depressants and died before her trial. At the nurses inquest, it was ruled that her death was accidental and not suicide.

An inquiry published in 2010 stated that it was unlikely that the nurse had set out to deliberately poisoned the three women and found that there was a catalogue of systemic failures in the way she was allowed to carry out her work. The inquiry stated that the decision to prosecute the nurse was the right one but that when they went through the clinical records that she had kept, the charts and notes, it was found that her records were entirely open and that the events that had occurred were instead the result of a combination of individual and systems failure.

June Driver, 67, died in July 2000. She was being treated for an infection after a hip replacement.

Eva Blackburn, 75, died in November 2001.

Annie Midgley, 96, died in July 2002. She had been admitted to hospital with abdominal pain.

The nurse had also been charged with attempting to murder another man aged 42 in June 2002 and had been charged with 13 counts of unlawfully administering poison to 12 other patients.

Dwayne Jonathon Bertrand

Age: 21

Sex: male

Date: 31 Oct 2001

Place: London

The death of Dwayne Jonathon Bertrand was reported as undetected by the Metropolitan Police in a Freedom of Information request.

No further information is known.

Nana Osei-Agyapong

Age: 25

Sex: male

Date: 31 Oct 2001

Place: Golden Square, Soho, London

Nana Osei-Agyapong was shot in his car outside the Kabaret Night Club in Upper John Street, London.

He had been to a private party at the club and at 3am had left to get his silver Renault Megane car to drive his friends home. However, as he went to get his car an argument started outside the club and a man shot him through the window of his car.

Nana Osei-Agyapong managed to drive off but was found 20 minutes later slumped in his car in Golden Square and was taken to University College Hospital where he died 30 minutes later.

He had been shot once in the chest.

At the time he had been wearing a blue and grey jacket, a dark blue t-shirt, blue denim jeans, a black belt that had a metal 'Iceberg' jeans logo on the buckle, white trainers with a thick blue flash on the sides and 'Prada' on the heel in red. He had also been wearing a heavy thick white metal necklace, which had a linked cross with a white stone in the middle of the cross and a thick metal lynx type bracelet.

A 25-year old man was arrested in relation to his murder in 2004 but was released without charge.

Nana Osei-Agyapong was a media student.

Dwayne Bertram

Age: 21

Sex: male

Date: 30 Oct 2001

Place: Bloomsbury, London

Dwayne Bertram was shot in his car in Bloomsbury.

He was unemployed and from Holloway.

Bill Chivers

Age: 86

Sex: male

Date: 29 Oct 2001

Place: Walters Avenue, Swffryd, Wales

Bill Chivers died after being mugged.

He was attacked after leaving the Swffryd Community Centre where he had been playing bingo on 15 September 2001. He was taken to the Royal Gwent Hospital in Newport where he died six weeks later. He suffered from hip, pelvis and arm injuries during the attack and later developed complications and died.

A 15-year-old teenager was tried for his murder but was acquitted. It was said that he had mugged Bill Chivers for a portion of pie and peas that he had bought. He denied the murder and said that he was at his nan's house for the whole time.

Mohammed Basharat

Age: 33

Sex: male

Date: 20 Oct 2001

Place: Little Horton Taxis, Park Lane, Little Horton, Bradford

Mohammed Basharat was shot at Little Horton Taxis where he worked in Park Lane, Little Horton, Bradford, at 8pm.

He was shot twice in the head by a man with a .38 calibre handgun.

His murder was described as exact and clinical and it was noted that no words were spoken.

He had been involved in a minor scuffle the day before at 6pm with a man described as of African-Caribbean appearance who had been driving a Renault Clio with another man when their wing mirrors had touched.

Mohammed Basharat had been driving his Vauxhall Cavalier car at the time. During the scuffle Mohammed Basharat had been forced to restrain a man who then threatened to kill him. They left their car behind and walked off but shouted to Mohammed Basharat, 'you don't know who you are messing with. I'm going to kill you'.

The police said the description of the man that had shot Mohammed Basharat was similar to the description of the man that Mohammed Basharat had had the scuffle with the day before. The gunman was said to have been about 5ft 9ins tall, slim and wearing a dark coloured anorak, a pair of black jeans, and a balaclava or scarf over his face. It was thought that he might have been wearing gloves too.

After shooting Mohammed Basharat, the man was said to have pointed the gun at other members of staff who said they heard the gun click, after which the gunman left.

In December 2014, a man that was currently serving a prison sentence for a shooting in the United States was identified as a prime suspect in Mohammed Basharat's murder and it was said that arrangements were being made to extradite him to the United

Kingdom to face trial. The extradition order was said to be the first of its kind since the 2003 US-UK bilateral extradition treaty which was ratified in 2007 and allowed either country to apply for a serving prisoner to be extradited to stand trial in that country with the agreement that, after the conclusion of the trial, they return to the original country to serve the rest of their sentence.

The man had been living in Little Horton and Girlington at the time of the murder and had regularly gone to the Young Lions Club in Lumb Lane, and at the time had refused to speak to the police.

Mohammed Basharat had been a taxi driver for 14 years. He was 6ft 5in tall.

Sukhabir Pattuwala

Age: 25

Sex: male

Date: 20 Oct 2001

Place: Great West Road, London

Sukhabir Pattuwala was shot at a restaurant on Great West Road.

He was shot in the head.

He had been out celebrating a friend's birthday.

Gilbert Wynter

Age: 40

Sex: male

Date: 18 Oct 2001

Place: London

The death of Gilbert Wynter was declared undetected in a Metropolitan Police Freedom Of Information request.

No further information is known.

The Freedom Of Information request states that he was 40 years of age and Afro-Caribbean and died on 18 October 2001, however, there is another Gilbert Wynter who was said to have vanished in 1998 and it is not clear whether or not this is a different Gilbert Wynter.

Raymond Isaacs

Age: 21

Sex: male

Date: 16 Oct 2001

Place: Hounslow, Middlesex

Raymond Isaacs was attacked in the street by up to ten other people.

Several people were convicted of lesser offences, but no one was convicted of his murder.

He was punched, kicked and stabbed outside a Nando's and a Kentucky Fried Chicken restaurant on Hounslow High Street and taken to the Middlesex University Hospital but died from a stab wound to the heart an hour and a half later. He had also been stabbed in the leg.

Raymond Isaacs had been to a cafe with his girlfriend, child and two friends in Hounslow on 16 October 2001. When Raymond Isaacs and one of his friends left to make a telephone call from a public phone box, it was said that one of his attackers started to stare at him and that there were then several confrontations between them.

Then, a man picked up a two to three feet long piece of wooden fencing and swung it at Raymond Isaacs.

It was said then that the man Raymond Isaacs was fighting then used his mobile phone to call in some other friends who arrived soon after with weapons.

There were then about 11 people attacking Raymond Isaacs and his friend. His friend managed to get into the cafe, but Raymond Isaacs ran off, but was caught outside a Nando's restaurant on the High Street where he was punched, kicked and stabbed.

It was said at one point that he had been surrounded by at least six people who were seen attacking him in a flurry of arms and legs.

The attack on him was said to have lasted only 15 seconds before the attackers dispersed.

Raymond Isaacs was left hanging over some railings. When his girlfriend arrived, she found him slumped on the pavement.

Brian Metcalfe

Age: 43

Sex: male

Date: 14 Oct 2001

Place: Station Road, Wath, Rotherham

Brian Metcalfe was beaten to death on wasteland under a railway bridge near a car park close by Station Road in Wath.

His body was found by a dog walker on 14 October 2001 shortly after 5pm after lying there for about two days. The carpark and railway bridge were near to Wath Rubber and Plastics.

The police said that they thought that he had been kicked to death and described the attack as apparently motiveless.

Brian Metcalfe last called a friend on Friday 12 October 2001 at about 2am and it was thought that he had been killed later that morning. He had been out drinking in pubs around Wath. The medical evidence suggested that he had died before 8am on the Friday but there was an unconfirmed sighting of him on the Saturday, 13 October 2001 and the police said that they were interested in hearing from anyone else that had seen him.

It was thought that he might have known the person that attacked him and that the answers to his murder probably lay in the local community.

A man was arrested soon after his body was found but he was released without charge.

His cause of death was given as blunt trauma to the chest, as a result of an assault. It was said that he had been kicked and had suffered multiple injuries as well as receiving a blow to the chest that had caused his heart to stop.

Brian Metcalfe was described as a loner and a quiet man who rarely went out and who preferred to socialise at home with his friends. The police said that they were trying to determine why Brian Metcalfe might have been out on the Saturday night. He was also a bachelor.

Further investigation found that he had been seen with a woman in Wath a week before he died. Also, reports were made of sightings of some people near the car park over the weekend that he died.

He had been wearing black denim jeans and a black leather jacket.

Tyrone Rowe

Age: 18

Sex: male

Date: 11 Oct 2001

Place: Caradon Way, Tottenham, North London

Tyrone Rowe was shot in Tottenham while in a car with three friends on 7 October 2001.

They had been in a battered red Ford Fiesta car at around 1.30am looking for a party when they encountered a group of six or seven black men in Caradon Way who drove up to them, two of whom then shot at them with hand guns. Tyrone Rowe was shot in the head and died in the Royal Free Hampstead Hospital on 11 October 2001. The driver of the red Ford Fiesta car was also shot in the chest but survived. He had managed to stagger two miles to an address whilst bleeding heavily and was then himself taken to a hospital but discharged himself the following day.

The gunmen had fired a total of eleven shots. Before firing the shots, the men were said to have calmly walked up to the battered red Ford Fiesta car.

It was said then that three of the black men then drove off in what was thought to have been a green Chrysler Voyager people carrier car, off along Turnpike Lane. The men were said to have been wearing hoods.

Police said that they were looking for a vital witness that was seen in the area who they described as black, aged about 30-years of age and wearing a three-quarter length black leather jacket.

It was thought that the shooting might have been a case of mistaken identity.

John Marzetti

Age: 45

Sex: male

Date: 11 Oct 2001

Place: The Coppins, New Addington, Croydon

John Marzetti was shot as he was changing a tyre on his car in a car park in The Coppins.

He was a second-hand-car dealer and had been changing the wheel on his BMW in a car park near his home in New Addington.

He was shot several times at about 6.15pm.

Police said that a suspect had been seen earlier on and it was thought that he might have been waiting for John Marzetti. He was described as black, wearing a hooded top and to have been wearing dark clothing and a puffa jacket.

Tony Lawlor

Age: 45

Sex: male

Date: 11 Oct 2001

Place: Middlemass Hey, Netherley, Liverpool

Tony Lawlor was shot dead outside some shops in Netherley.

He was shot several times in the back.

His murder was witnessed by his mother who said that the gunman shot him repeatedly and then leaned over him to check that he was dead. his mother chased the gunman and hit him with her shopping bag.

The gunman was said to have been dressed in black.

Four men had jumped out of a blue Ford Transit van as Tony Lawlor got out of his car near a chip shop at the Middlemass Hey shopping parade in Netherley at 6.30pm and chased him and shot him down as he crossed over some waste ground.

The blue Ford Transit van was later found burnt out in Woolton Park at the junction with Winhill in Liverpool.

It was thought that Tony Lawlor had been shot with a .38 revolver.

An 11-year-old boy was also shot in the leg by a stray bullet during the shooting.

The shooting was said to have been the result of an incident in a bar earlier in which someone was disrespected. the incident was said to have set off a feud between two families.

Tony Lawlor's brother, Stephen Lawlor, was himself also shot dead some months earlier in May 2002 after leaving a party although a man was convicted for his murder in 2002. However, soon after, while the man that was charged with shooting Tony Lawlor's brother was on remand awaiting trial for murder, the man's brother, Ian Clarke, was shot and killed in September 2001 in Tuebrook. Ian Clarke's murder is also currently unsolved.

John Hall and David McIntosh

Age: 45 and 35

Sex: male and male

Date: 3 Oct 2001

Place: Larkhall, Lanarkshire

John Hall and David McIntosh were found dead on a dirt track in Larkhall in 2001.

They had been involved in small time car crime but later moved into drugs. However, it was said that after cocaine worth £120,000 was seized by the police and they failed to pay for it they were both shot in the head.

They were described as petty criminals that had blundered out of their depth.

They had taken five kilograms of cocaine which they intended to cut and then sell on and had ordered a small-time drug dealer who owed them thousands of pounds to hide it at his workplace, NTL in Livingston, West

Lothian. However, the man was caught with the drugs and sent to prison in December 2000 for six years.

However, John Hall and David McIntosh were put under increasing pressure to pay for the drugs.

Then, on 3 October 2001 John Hall and David McIntosh were found dead in an old scrapyard near to a go-karting arena, Summerlee raceway, in Merryton Road and close to the M74 after having last been seen at the Gretna greyhound track at 8pm. David McIntosh's black Volkswagen Golf car, registration number X468 ABV, was found burned out nearby.

Police said that they were interested in speaking to anyone that had seen the car between 6pm on the Tuesday 2 October 2001 and the afternoon of 3 October 2001 when their bodies were found. They had both left their respective homes at 6pm to go out for a social night together. They were found at 4.20pm on 3 October by a female pensioner who had been out for a walk.

They had been seen at the greyhound track in Gretna at 8pm and it was thought that they had left between 9pm and 10pm. It was said that the journey from their homes to the greyhound track was a two hour one and that they would have taken the M74 and on the return journey would have come off at Larkhall and then taken the Hamilton Road towards the Go-Kart circuit and then down the track into the disused scrap yard. The site was dark and noted for its isolated location and seclusion.

They had both been shot through the head in the car at close range. Their bodies were found close to one another and had been dowsed in petrol and burned with the car.

When the police went to see the man that had lost the cocaine in prison and told him that John Hall and David McIntosh had been found shot dead, they said that he knew immediately who had done it and why. It was said that the main suspect was another car criminal that had subsequently emerged to become a successful criminal known for his violence and involvement in the gang wars in Paisley. The man was said to have started off like John Hall and David McIntosh in the stolen car market and to have had a similar interest in greyhound racing.

The police said that John Hall had recently been charged with being part of a £140,000 car crime ring that was stealing and selling cars with false registration plates and identification numbers but the trial, which was due to take place at Hamilton Sheriff Court in April 2000 collapsed due to lack of evidence and legal complications over European human rights laws. He had denied the charges.

The police said that there was a possibility that their murders could be linked to the murders of William Lindsay and John Henry Nisbet who were found shot and set on fire in a field in Elphinstone, Tranent in 1999.

At the time they were both unemployed.

Dean Eccleston

Age: 24

Sex: male

Date: 1 Oct 2001

Place: Shakespeare Walk, Chorlton-on-Medlock

Dean Eccleston was shot seven times in Shakespeare Walk as he left a friend's house.

He had been wearing a bullet proof vest at the time. His mother later noted that he also used to sleep with a gun under his pillow.

His mother said that she knew who the gunmen were but said that witnesses were too scared to come forward. She said that they were members of the Gooch Close Gang.

It was noted that Dean Eccleston's friend, who had been with him at the time he was shot, didn't attend the inquest. Dean Eccleston's mother said that the man had given her the names of the men that had shot Dean Eccleston but would not make a statement to the police naming them. A detective sergeant said that if the man had given them the names of the men involved then they would probably have been able to prosecute them.

The inquest heard that there had been a large police investigation into his murder that had involved 28,000 man-hours and that 195 statements were taken.

It was noted that although Dean Eccleston had previously spent time in prison, he had not been a member of the Longsight Crew.

Patrick Erhabor

Age: 5

Sex: male

Date: 21 Sep 2001

Place: River Thames, London

The torso of Patrick Erhabor was found dead in the River Thames on 21 September 2001 near Tower Bridge and the Globe Theatre.

At the time he was unidentified and known only as 'Adam', but in early February 2013 he was identified by a woman in Nigeria as Patrick Erhabor. She said that she used to look after him in Germany before he was brought illegally into the United Kingdom. She had been living in Glasgow in 2002.

Police said that they thought that he had been murdered during a ritual sacrifice and that he had been drugged beforehand with a black magic potion. It was found that his body had contained traces of Calabar bean which would have left him paralysed but conscious when his throat was cut.

It was suggested that the murder was similar to the muti sacrifices carried out in the sub-Saharan African region where it was thought that the body parts of children were sacred.

His head, arms and legs had all been expertly cut off.

His post mortem stated that he had been drugged and had then had his throat slit and his blood drained after which his head and limbs were expertly cut off.

The only clothes he had on were a pair of orange shorts which were determined to be sold exclusively in Woolworths in Germany and Austria.

Forensic analysis that used techniques to analyse radioactive isotopes showed that Patrick Erhabor was from the Benin City area of Nigeria which was noted as being the birthplace of voodoo.

The woman that had identified Patrick Erhabor had been in Glasgow in 2002 and the police had questioned her but there was no evidence against her and because of her mental state she was deported back to Nigeria. When she was arrested, the police found clothing in the Glasgow flat that was similar to the clothing worn by Patrick Erhabor.

The woman said that she had been looking after him in Germany but had handed him over to a man who had then taken him to the United Kingdom.

It was thought that Patrick Erhabor was murdered a few days after arriving in the United Kingdom.

A woman that had initially been questioned later spoke to reporters in 2011 when she said that she had given Patrick Erhabor to a man in Hamburg who she incorrectly named and showed reporters a photo and gave Patrick Erhabor a false name. At the time she said little else about the case but in 2013 she decided to reveal everything that she knew, and reporters flew out to Benin City in Nigeria to interview her. She then revealed Patrick Erhabor's true name and said that the previous photo she had shown in 2011 was not Patrick Erhabor, but that of another friend's child. When she was asked who have killed Patrick Erhabor she said a 'group of people'. She said, 'They used him for a ritual in the water.'.

At the 2011 interview she had named a man that she had given the child to by way of a nickname but in 2013 she revealed his full name. The man was later identified as a bogus asylum seeker who had come to London in 1997. However, when he was questioned over the murder he said that he knew nothing. The man had been arrested in 2002 at which time the police had found a plastic bag, a mixture of bone, sand and flecks of gold very similar to a sample found in Patrick Erhabor's stomach, at the man's house.

Police also found a video in his house titled 'Rituals' which contained a B-movie in which a man cuts off another man's head.

However, the man said that the items had belonged to other people in the house and the police said that they were unable to establish a link between him and the items.

The man was convicted for people smuggling in 2004 and sentenced to four and a half years and whilst in prison he contacted the police saying that he wanted to help with the investigation, but it was determined that he was wasting police time and he was later deported back to Nigeria.

Whilst the police said that the information that the woman gave in 2013 was a development and connected the Nigerian man previously questioned with the crime, the police said that she had proven to have been unreliable in the past and said that she had psychiatric problems. It was noted that in 2013 she was taking medication. She had earlier given a photo to the police who she said was a picture of Patrick Erhabor but it was later proved not to be him.

Investigators also went to Hamburg in Germany where the woman had lived and spoke to some people that remembered her and the child.

Another Nigerian suspect was arrested in 2003 in Dublin, but no charges were made.

Geoff Gray

Age: 17

Sex: male

Date: 17 Sep 2001

Place: Deepcut Barracks, Surrey

Geoff Gray died from two bullet wounds to his head.

He had been on night-time guard duty at the time he was shot at the Deepcut Barracks.

The British Army said that he shot himself twice in the head, but his family have said that there was evidence that another soldier had fired the weapon and that that evidence was later destroyed.

It was said that a man was seen running away from where his body was found and that his body had been moved after he was shot dead. It was also heard that a soldier had been found to have had a warm gun after the shooting, indicating that it had recently been fired but that it was not looked into any further. A witness that had seen the scene said that it was consistent with third-party involvement.

A ballistics expert said that he thought that it was highly unlikely that Geoff Gray had shot himself.

In 2002 an open verdict was returned but on 2006 a review, known as the Blake review, stated that he committed suicide.

His death was one of a number of mysterious deaths at the barracks over several years.

In 2014, it was said that the army had refused to release documents associated with the case and requested that the family that wanted them carry out a freedom of information request, although adding that they would have to pay for it as the £600 cap on free requests would be exceeded.

In 2017 it was heard that the family could apply for a fresh inquest after the family applied to the High Court stating that new evidence had come to light. They had been given 16,000 pages of previously unseen evidence. It was noted that the original inquest had had 20 pages of evidence to work with and had lasted four hours.

His mother also said that her lawyers had witness statements that named the person responsible for shooting Geoff Gray.

However, the fresh inquest returned a verdict of suicide on 20 June 2019.

He was from Seaham in County Durham.

Ian Clarke

Age: 32

Sex: male

Date: 13 Sep 2001

Place: Tuebrook, Liverpool

Ian Clarke was shot as he sat in his car at some traffic lights outside the Newsham Pub in Tuebrook. He died five days later in hospital at 10.45pm on 13 September 2001.

He was a doorman at the Barcelona bar in the city centre and had worked for Premier Security and was shot as he drove to work on the Saturday at 10pm, 8 September 2001.

A dark Ford Mondeo car was seen to pull up alongside his car at the traffic lights from which a number of shots were then fired. He had at least four gunshot wounds. It was thought that the Ford Mondeo car had done a U-turn after the first volley of shots before firing again.

After the shooting, the Ford Mondeo car drove off at speed towards Breck Road and was later found burned out in Redbrook Street, Anfield.

Ian Clarke was shot after his younger brother was arrested for the murder of a man who was shot in May 2001 and the following month, the man's brother, Tony Lawlor was also shot, a murder which is currently also unsolved. The police said that they were looking into the connection that his murder was a revenge attack for the murder of the man in May 2001 and that he had been shot by a hired professional.

It was thought that his murder had been associated with a gang war to control the nightclub security business across Merseyside.

Although Ian Clarke did not have a criminal record, the police said that he was known to them.

Lindsey Chezine Scholes

Age: 17

Sex: female

Date: 8 Sep 2001

Place: 86 Millgate Street, Royston, Barnsley

Lindsey Chezine Scholes died from smoke inhalation after the house that she was staying in was set on fire.

The fire was started at 4.30am on 8 September 2001. She had been staying with some friends at the house on the first floor at the time where a party had been held and was rescued from the fire by firemen. However, she had already received burns and been exposed to the smoke and fumes.

She was taken to Barnsley District Hospital where she was found to have 18% burns and then taken to the Royal Hallamshire for further treatment but died on 10 September 2001.

The police said that accelerants had been used to start the fire which was started at the front door of the property. The fire then spread through the house and two other girls that had been asleep upstairs escaped through a window but Lindsey Scholes, who was unconscious, was in the house until the firemen arrived.

It was thought that Lindsey Scholes might have known the people that had started the fire.

A number of people were arrested but no one was ever charged.

There had been a party at the house earlier on in the night and a number of young local people had been attending.

Yasser Nazir

Age: 16

Sex: male

Date: 5 Sep 2001

Place: Haworth Road, Chellow Heights, Bradford

Yasser Nazir was shot twice in the head in Haworth Road in what was said to have been an execution-style shooting relating to an earlier assault.

He had been sitting in a white Vauxhall Astra car on the forecourt of a Shell petrol station in Haworth Road, Bradford, with two other friends on 5 September 2001 when a green Honda Accord car pulled up and a passenger in the car shot Yasser Nazir with a long-barrelled shotgun. Yasser Nazir then managed to drive about 100 yards up the road before he collapsed and died. The green Honda Accord car had followed him and when it caught up the passenger shot Yasser Nazir again. His two friends then ran off.

After the shooting the green Honda Accord car did a U-turn and sped off towards Toller Lane.

He had been driving the white Vauxhall Astra car illegally and had earlier attended a police station in Bradford in relation to an earlier assault in which some people were ambushed and attacked with hammers, axes and knives.

Shortly before Yasser Nazir pulled into the petrol station after leaving the police station a red Mercedes-Benz car that had been in front of his had started to swerve across the road after which Yasser Nazir pulled into the petrol station and then the green Honda Accord car pulled up and he was shot.

It was thought that the shooting was gang related and had been a tit-for-tat attack in revenge for an assault a month earlier in the summer of 2001 on a senior gang member in which a man was injured.

On the day of his murder, Yasser Nazir and his two friends had been to the police station to attend some identity parades. However, Yasser Nazir had refused to take part in the identity parades but had driven his two friends there. However, when they arrived his two other friends also refused to take part in the identification parades and they all left together. It was thought then that the people involved in the incident who had been at the police station had called other people on their mobile phones to say that Yasser Nazir was at the police station and that Yasser Nazir had then been followed by some people in cars. His brother was later convicted of conspiracy to murder in 2003 for the earlier incident for which Yasser Nazir and his friends had gone to the police station about.

The green Honda Accord car was later found burned out, but the gun was never found.

Ten people were arrested in relation to the shooting, but no one was charged due to a lack of evidence.

Yasser Nazir was said to have been a drug dealer.

His brother had said that he thought that it had been a case of mistaken identity.

Yasser Nazir had lived in Chatsworth Street, Keighley.

Naziat Parveen Zafar

Age: 38

Sex: female

Date: 26 Aug 2001

Place: Streatham, South London

Naziat Parveen Zafar was killed at her home in front of her children.

Her husband was the main suspect and was believed to have fled to Pakistan in 2001.

Naziat Khan's two daughters said that they were in the room when their mother was strangled and saw him do it.

Naziat Zafar was strangled in her home with a scarf. Her daughters said that after she died their father warned them that they would be next.

It was said that he had strangled her after she asked him for a divorce. They had had an arranged marriage.

His children said that the father used to beat Naziat Zafar and never contributed financially to the family and he was asked to leave, and they had separated.

One of her daughters said that she had been to a neighbour's house to read Arabic after which she went home, having a key to get in. She said that when she got home she found her father at the door covered in scratches and said that she knew something was wrong. She said that when she went in she saw her mother lying on the floor with her eyes closed and said that she looked like she was struggling to breathe. She said that one of her other sisters was in the corner and looked pale and was shaking and that her father then locked the door behind her. She said that her sister then became hysterical and started to scream and that her father rushed at her and started pulling her scarf but that she managed to pull him away from her sister after which her father went to her mother who was lying on the floor. She said that her mother had blood gushing out of her but looked conscious but that her father then pulled the ends of her scarf and strangled her in front of them.

She said that after killing their mother, her father then turned round to them and told them that he would do the same to them if they told anyone what he had done.

She said that their father then took jewellery off of Naziat Zafar and took them out of the house. She said that they walked around for ages with their father who told them that they couldn't breathe a word about what he had done to anyone or else he would kill them.

She said that her father then took them to one of his friends' houses and left them there. She said that she kept calling her home to speak to her mother and said that the next day her father called her to say that he was with their mother and everything was alright.

However, she said that the next day the police came and told her that her mother was dead and that their father had fled to Pakistan. Naziat Zafar's body was found by her 16-year-old son after he returned from a trip to Bradford with his uncle.

His daughter later said that she thought that her father deliberately planned for her 16-year-old brother to go to Bradford so that he would be out of the way.

The daughter said that she and her brothers and sisters were then put into foster care and that sometime later she heard on the grapevine that her father was living in his home village of Rawalpindi in Pakistan. However, there was no extradition treaty between the UK and Pakistan and the police were unable to arrest the father. The police did say that they had been given permission by the Crown Prosecution Service to arrest the father should he ever return to England.

Carlton McDonald

Age: 21

Sex: male

Date: 26 Aug 2001

Place: Camberwell New Road, Camberwell

Carlton McDonald was stabbed to death in Camberwell New Road by a gang of about 15 black youths.

He was found slumped in an alleyway. He had been stabbed once and was taken to King's College Hospital where he died an hour later.

He had been out in Camberwell to a wedding reception at St. Mary's Community Hall on the Sunday night. He had gone home when it was said that he got a call from a friend saying that he had been robbed and had lost his phone and Carlton McDonald agreed to go and meet him at the corner of Warner Road.

He was later walking along Camberwell New Road with four friends in the early hours when they were attacked by the gang of 15 youths who were armed with knives, a baseball bat and a hammer.

His four friends were all also injured and taken to hospital but discharged soon after.

Around the same time, another man was robbed by a gang of youths and reported the incident to the police.

Both the murder and the robbery happened between midnight and 1.30am on 26 August 2001.

It was thought that the 15 gang members had all been aged between 15 and 18 years old. It was thought that they had carried out a string of robberies and assaults from midnight onwards and the police said that they were interested in hearing from anyone else that had been robbed or assaulted. it was also said that the gang might have been high on drugs at the time.

Police found two kitchen knives in the area but said that they didn't think they had been the murder weapons.

Three people were arrested the following day, but none were charged.

Carlton McDonald had worked at a West Indian bakery, the Mixed Blessings Bakery, on Mitcham Road in Tooting since leaving school. The police said that he was not involved with either gangs or drugs.

Frederick Baker

Age: 63

Sex: male

Date: 26 Aug 2001

Place: Woodside Road, Caddington, Luton, Bedfordshire

Frederick Baker died after being physically assaulted in Woodside near Caddington, Luton.

He had been hit over the head with a large piece of wood and died the following day.

He had been involved in a fight.

Patrick Pasipanodya

Age: 29

Sex: male

Date: 22 Aug 2001

Place: Picketts Lock Lane, Edmonton

Patrick Pasipanodya was shot in a drive-by shooting.

He had been in his blue VW Golf car at the time.

The police said that they were looking to speak to two people that were seen on motor scooters around the time that he was shot. They were seen at the corner of Advent Way and Lee Park Way in Edmonton.

The first motor scooter rider was described as white, between 5ft 8ins and 5ft 10ins tall, of medium build and wearing light blue jeans, a thin, dark, lightweight jacket and white trainers. The riders crash helmet was white and full faced and might have had a pattern or transfer on it. The bike was a newish looking, 1-year old, red Peugeot or Piaggio motor scooter, about 80cc to 125cc in size.

The second motor scooter rider was described as white, between 5ft 8ins and 5ft 10ins tall, of medium build, wearing dark tracksuit bottoms and white trainers. The rider had been wearing a black full faced helmet and had been riding a dark coloured newish looking, 1-year old, red Peugeot or Piaggio motor scooter, about 80cc to 125cc in size.

The police said that they were not thought of as suspects, but it was thought that they might have seen something that could have helped with their enquiries.

Patrick Pasipanodya had been a television actor and was also a doorman.

Martin Silvester

Age: 34

Sex: male

Date: 21 Aug 2001

Place: Pikehelve Street, Wednesbury, West Midlands

Martin Silvester was shot whilst sat in his car outside his business in Pikehelve Street, Wednesbury just before midnight on 21 August 2001.

The main suspect was a man that had been tried and convicted for conspiracy to rob a post office in 1997 but who had escaped from Birmingham Crown Court and gone on the run. It was thought that he had shot Martin Silvester, but he was not found until 6 January 2004 when the police carried out an armed raid at a house in Shenstone, near Lichfield, Staffordshire where he was staying with an associate. He was then taken to HMP Woodhill where he hanged himself on 19 January 2004.

Martin Silvester was a haulage contractor from Tipton in the West Midlands and ran Wednesbury Logistical Services.

He was pistol whipped as he sat in his car and then shot in the chest. Although he was shot, Martin Silvester managed to drive several hundred meters into Bagnall Street before crashing outside the Miners Arms pub. The bullet had gone through his heart.

Martin Silvester was an ex-soldier.

Michael James Cabey

Age: 28

Sex: male

Date: 5 Aug 2001

Place: Rossington Street, Clapton

Michael Cabey was shot at the corner of Rossington Street and Northwold Road in Clapton on 5 August 2001 in a drive by shooting.

Witnesses saw three men in a black Ford Fiesta 1.3LX car registration R160 ULD from which the shots were fired out of an open window. He was sitting on a wall at the time with two friends.

The black Ford Fiesta car then drove off towards Clapton Road.

He had been hit four times.

An ambulance was called and Michael Cabey was taken to Homerton hospital but was pronounced dead on arrival.

The police said that they were interested in speaking to a well-dressed black woman who was thought to have picked up Michael Cabey's phone after he was shot. The police said that they had been unable to find it. It was said that she had picked it up whilst members of the public were helping Michael Cabey and had then said that it was hers and walked off.

Michael Cabey worked at a supermarket.

Phillip Saville

Age: 40

Sex: male

Date: 2 Aug 2001

Place: Wardour Street, Soho, London

Phillip Saville was killed in Wardour Street, London, on 2 August 2001.

He had become involved in a late-night fight, possibly involving six men, whilst out at a leaving party for a work colleague. He was taken to the St Mary's Hospital and then later transferred to the private Wellington Hospital in St Johns Wood, London where he died 16 days later on 18 August 2001.

The fight had taken place outside a bar.

A man was charged with murder, but the charge was dropped due to insufficient evidence. It was heard that Phillip Saville was pushed and had hit his head on the ground after hitting a man with a broken bottle.

Phillip Saville had suffered a fractured skull. His cause of death was stated as being an injury to his head.

Phillip Saville was a director of a soil investigation drilling company.

Jimmy Millen

Age: 27

Sex: male

Date: 1 Aug 2001

Place: Tile Barn Road, Hastings

Jimmy Millen was shot by two men on a motorbike in Tile Barn Road, Hastings whilst he was in the street working on a car.

He was shot four times in the back at close range but managed to crawl to Carpenter Drive where he was found and taken to Conquest Hospital in an ambulance where he later died.

A witness said that the man on the motorbike that had fire the shot had been wearing black and the police later said that both men on the bike had been wearing black motorcycle leathers and helmets with blacked-out visors. After the shooting, the motorbike was said to have driven off in the direction of the Castleham industrial estate.

His murder was thought to have been linked to the murder of Jason Martin-Smith 28 who was abducted in August 2001. Jason Martin-Smith's body has never been found but a man was convicted for his murder in 2015 and sentenced to 29 years. It was thought that Jason Martin-Smith had been taken to a lock-up where he was dismembered in relation to a £200,000 drugs debt.

The police said that it was during the investigation into Jimmy Millen's murder that details of Jason Martin-Smith's murder came to light.

A man was arrested on suspicion of conspiracy to murder Jimmy Millen in February 2015, but no trial results are known.

Jimmy Millen was a boxer and a doorman. His family said that they thought that his murderers lived locally and added that she didn't think that the police had looked deeply into his case because he had had a criminal record.

It was also thought that Jimmy Millen had known James Ashley who was shot dead by the police at his house in Hastings in 1998.

Jimmy Millen had lived in Taylors Close in Hastings at the time, not far from Tile Barn Road.

He had three children.

Makram Abdul-Kadir

Age: unknown

Sex: male

Date: 28 Jul 2001

Place: Inverness Terrace, Bayswater

Makram Abdul-Kadir died in a fire. He was sleeping rough in a car that someone set on fire.

A man was tried for his murder but acquitted. He had denied starting the fire and it was noted that the evidence against him was circumstantial.

Makram Abdul-Kadir had been sleeping in an abandoned car in an underground car park in Inverness Terrace, Bayswater in July 2001. Firemen were called after black smoke was seen coming out of the garages and when they extinguished the flames they found the body of Makram Abdul-Kadir lying on the back seat.

His post-mortem stated that his cause of death was smoke inhalation.

The man that was charged with his murder was also homeless but denied murder and arson. He was found near the scene when the firemen arrived and was seen to be mumbling incoherently. When he was questioned he refused to answer any questions.

It was thought that Makram Abdul-Kadir had been asleep in the car when it was set on fire. He had had 308mg of alcohol per 100ml of blood in his system which equated to being about three times over the drink drive limit.

Fire investigators said that the fire had started in the front seat and said that they thought that it was unlikely that Makram Abdul-Kadir had started it by falling asleep with a lit cigarette.

Makram Abdul-Kadir was homeless and was a Somalian national. it was said that very little was known about him, including his age, when he had come to the UK or whether he had any family in the country.

Andrew Chubb

Age: 58

Sex: male

Date: 27 Jul 2001

Place: Leigh, Chard, Somerset

Andrew Chubb was killed in an explosion in his garden shed. His death was determined to be unascertained.

The verdict at his first inquest ruled that his death had been accidental. However, a second inquest was carried out in 2007 and his death was determined to have been unascertained, overturning the verdict of accidental death.

He died shortly after he asked his wife for a divorce. He had been having an affair with a 37-year-old woman in Portsmouth where he worked as a judge and would go home to his wife at the weekends to their house near Ford Abbey in Somerset. He had told her about his affair after a woman called his house in Leigh and asked for him but had hung up when she had asked who was speaking. However, it was said that he had told his wife that he was planning to end the affairs and had no intention of leaving her.

On the day he died he had got home at 7.30pm and asked his wife for a divorce and then gone out into the garden shed in his gardening clothes. His wife said that she saw him soon after in the garden shed standing over a motorised lawnmower after which she said that she went back into the house. She said that she then heard an explosion at 8.50pm.

The garden shed had contained a sit-on lawnmower and also petrol and fuel for a strimmer.

It was said that the fire that he died in was caused or accelerated by the ignition of petrol vapour.

It was suggested that a spark from the lawnmower had ignited the petrol and caused an explosion and a fireball.

It was said that it was a mystery why he had shut the shed door and not tried to escape.

A fireman that was called out to the fire said that when he found Andrew Chubb's body, the fire did seem suspicious but that his inspections showed no obvious signs of foul play. When asked about loud bangs that a neighbour had heard he said that they were probably caused by the asbestos in the shed as it burned.

Andrew Chubb didn't smoke or carry matches, and no one heard him try to start the lawnmower. It was noted that the shed didn't have any electricity or gas supply either.

His wife, who inherited his estate worth £1,000,000 moved to Australia after his death and it was said that a 'lingering cloud of suspicion' hung over her. However, judges at a high court said that there was not a shred of evidence to support a verdict of unlawful killing and a Lord Chief Justice said that it was possible that Andrew Chubb had killed himself.

A judge said that it would have been virtually impossible for his wife to have disabled Andrew Chubb in the shed and set him on fire.

His wife said that his mistress had been blackmailing him.

His mistress at the second inquest said that Andrew Chubb's death was not an accident. She said, 'I do not believe Andrew died accidentally or by his own hand.'.

Andrew Chubb's wife was arrested and questioned over Andrew Chubb's death in May 2002 but in September 2002 they said that they would not be charging her in connection with his death.

A pathologist who examined the original post-mortem at the 2007 inquest said that its results were insufficient, confusing and didn't make sense. He said that from the evidence in the findings it would have been impossible to conclude that Andrew Chubb had burned to death.

A friend of Andrew Chubb said that Andrew Chubb had disapproved of suicide so much so that he had not gone to the funeral of a friend that had killed himself.

Andrew Chubb had been in the navy for 20 years and before being appointed a judge on the western circuit he had been a barrister.

He had been married for 34 years.

Daniel Dale

Age: 18

Sex: male

Date: 25 Jul 2001

Place: Keele Close, Collyhurst, Manchester

Daniel Dale was shot in the back in Keele Close, Collyhurst.

He was found in an alleyway off of Farnborough Road.

It was said that the shooting was related to gang rivalry but also said that Daniel Dale was not involved with gangs, crime or drugs.

A man was convicted of his murder in 2002 but later, in 2014, his conviction was quashed after new forensic evidence was presented. The judge said that expert evidence might reasonably have affected the decision of the jury and his conviction was quashed.

He was killed the day after a murder trial that he was due to give evidence in finished. Daniel Dale had been due to give evidence in court regarding the death of a friend who was stabbed to death in Cheetham Hill but the person on trial pleaded guilty to the crime and Daniel Dale was not called. It was thought that his murder was not associated with the trial.

He had been talking to friends in Keele Close when he was shot in the back after a gunman fired into the group indiscriminately. The shot went through his heart and he died.

A Walther PPK self-loading pistol, said to have been the weapon used, was later found at the house of one of the men tried along with the man convicted.

The man that was initially convicted of Daniel Dale's murder was convicted in part due to particles found on a black Henri Lloyd hooded jacket found at his home under the stairs which were said to have been gunshot residue. It was said that the residue supported the assertion that he had been the gunman. However, some students who were studying the case stated that forensic analysis had improved since 2012 and that by using the latest techniques the evidence offered in the 2002 trial would not have been valid in a 2014 trial and as such the evidence had no value and his conviction was quashed. It was stated that what had been determined as gunshot residue in 2002 could well have been powder from a firework.

It was noted that in 2006 the Forensic Science Service issued new guidelines on the assessment, interpretation and reporting of firearms chemistry cases under which the amount of residue found on the black Henri Lloyd hooded jacket were so small that they could not be considered to have evidential value.

It was also said that the witness identification of the man who was convicted was weak and that the jury might have found that the gunshot residue forensic evidence was enough to support the prosecution's case and to return a guilty verdict. The case had also relied on voice identification evidence which was also considered questionable.

After his release from prison, the released man said, 'I partly feel responsible because it was my group of friends that was actually responsible for his murder.'.

The man tried for the murder of Daniel Dale had been tried alongside three other people, including his brother. One of the men tried had earlier pleaded guilty to possession of a firearm with intent to endanger life, possessing ammunition without a certificate, and assisting offenders and then gave evidence for the prosecution. Also, during the trial, one of the other men tried changed his plea and pleaded guilty to possessing a firearm with intent to endanger life. The third man was convicted of wounding with intent although his conviction was later quashed, and he was sentenced for possessing a firearm with intent.

Richie Clayton

Age: 30

Sex: male

Date: 25 Jul 2001

Place: Belgrave Road, Aigburth

Richie Clayton was shot on Belgrave Road just before 8pm on 25 July 2001.

His two attackers had pulled up in a green Ford Mondeo car outside a gym on Aigburth Road and had then chased him down Belgrave Road firing at him several times. The men had been wearing masks.

After being shot Richie Clayton managed to run to a nearby house but couldn't get in and then ran off to another house but then doubled back to the previous house where he collapsed and died. When he had got to the first house a man that had tried to help him was also shot in the leg.

After the shooting his attackers drove off along Belgrave Road and into Buckland

Street. The green Ford Mondeo car was later found burned out in a nearby cul-de-sac. It was thought that they had then run over a footbridge over the railway line at St Michael's station and then gone off through Priory Woods.

He had previously been working out at a gym on Aigburth Road in Aigburth several hours before he was shot but had gone back at around 8pm. He was seen outside the gym talking to another man when the green Ford Mondeo car pulled up.

Cherie Melgram

Age: 24

Sex: female

Date: 20 Jul 2001

Place: St Leonards Road, Girlington

Cherie Melgram was found on the floor in her house and later died in hospital. The cause of death was not determined.

She was found on the floor near her fireplace and taken to Bradford Royal Infirmary where she was pronounced dead on arrival.

She had had two children.

Hugh Scott

Age: 19

Sex: male

Date: 15 Jul 2001

Place: Hayfield Pub, Chapeltown, Leeds

Hugh Scott was shot in the abdomen at the back of the Hayfield Pub in Chapeltown on 14 July 2001.

He went to hospital but later died the next day on 15 July 2001.

He had been shot with a sub-machinegun.

A man was tried for his murder but acquitted after a key witness, one of the people shot with Hugh Scott, refused to give evidence.

Hugh Scott had been with three other men behind the pub at the time, and all of them were injured. The man that was tried for the murder of Hugh Scott was also tried for their attempted murders but similarly acquitted.

Oguzhin Ozdemir

Age: 26

Sex: male

Date: 14 Jul 2001

Place: River Lea, South Tottenham

Oguzhin Ozdemir was shot.

Three people were tried for his kidnap and murder and were convicted of kidnapping him but it could not be proven who had shot him and so they were all acquitted of the murder charge.

Oguzhin Ozdemir, who was Turkish, was said to be a small-time drug dealer selling heroin and it was thought that he had been murdered after he had lost some heroin that he had received from members of the Tottenham Mandem gang and had been unable to pay for it.

He was later found by anglers on a river bank in north London having been shot four times, twice in the head and twice in the back.

After he was murdered a man set fire to Oguzhin Ozdemir's car at a Muslim cemetery in Walthamstow, for which he was also convicted. Oguzhin Ozdemir's BMW car was seen on CCTV being driven to the cemetery.

It was said that Oguzhin Ozdemir had begged his friends to help get the money and that he had tried to escape his kidnappers. He had gone to meet the men that he owed the money to, said to be members of the Tottenham Mandem gang, in Tottenham on 14 July 2001 and whilst with them he had made a number of calls to friends to get the money during which one of the men had grabbed the phone and said that they were going to kill Oguzhin Ozdemir unless they got the goods or the money. However, one of Oguzhin Ozdemir's friends threatened to call the police and the men hung up.

Later on that night some anglers that were on an all-night carp fishing contest at a reservoir in Tottenham heard several gunshots.

Oguzhin Ozdemir had lived in Enfield.

Julie Foster

Age: 41

Sex: female

Date: 10 Jul 2001

Place: Stansted Road, Elsenham, Essex

Julie Foster was beaten to death in her home in Elsenham, Essex.

Her ex-boyfriend was tried for her murder but acquitted. He was arrested soon after the murder but released and then arrested again later and charged.

Her body was found at her home in her bedroom at 8.45pm on 10 July 2001 by her eight-year-old son when he went in to ask about breakfast. He had woken late and had realised that he was late for school. After finding her he called 999.

The son said that he had heard creaking footsteps climbing the stairs a few hours before he found her body and it was thought that he might have heard her murderer moving about in the house.

She had been beaten about the head with a blunt instrument and left lying naked in a pool of blood.

It was thought that she had been killed between midnight and 7am on 10 July 2001.

Police said that they found what they thought was the murder weapon.

She was known to drink in the Crooked House Pub and to have friends in Australia.

At the time of her murder the police said that they were looking for a physiotherapist that knew her that had lived in Wolverhampton.

Julie Foster ran a pet shop on the High Road in Thorndon and the police said at the time that they were looking to hear from bird food dealers who worked in the area.

The police said that they were also looking to hear from regulars at the Challenges Gym in Bishop's Stortford where she had been going.

The police said that they were also looking for an L or M registered transit style van that was seen on her road around the 9 and 10 July 2001 at about 2am.

They said that they were also interested in speaking to a man that was seen running along Station Road at about 6am on 10 July 2001 who was described as white, aged between 25 and 35 years old, with short fair hair and carrying a white plastic bag.

They also said that a third man was seen using a mobile phone in Leigh Road on two evenings at the beginning of July and then again later after 10 July. He was described as being in his mid-20s and as having short brown wavy hair.

The man that was tried for her murder was said to have been in a relationship with Julie Foster for three years, but that Julie Foster had ended it two weeks before her death saying that she didn't love him anymore. He was said to then have broken into her house in the night and beaten her to death with a cricket bat. The man had worked at Stanstead airport and police had canvassed the area with flyers during their investigation.

The man had called at Julie Foster's house later to collect some of his clothing and met Julie Foster's son who was crying and said to him 'Mummy's dead'.

They had first been childhood sweethearts and then met again later in 1997 when they began having a relationship around the time that Julie Foster left her husband.

Mithat Lleshi

Age: 23

Sex: male

Date: 7 Jul 2001

Place: Grosvenor Centre, Northampton

Mithat Lleshi was stabbed outside a shopping centre.

He was involved in a fight with six men on the walkway between the shopping centre and the bus station during which he was stabbed. He was found by a security guard who tried to give him first aid and was then taken to Northampton General Hospital were surgery was carried out but died six hours later.

A friend that he had been with who received three stab wounds to his backside survived and later went back to Albania. At Mithat Lleshi's inquest it was heard that the man had visited Mithat Lleshi's family and told them that he knew who had killed Mithat

Lleshi and that he would be seeking revenge.

CCTV footage showed a group of men in the Grosvenor Centre on the ground floor waiting and then asking the man outside. It was said that he first refused to go outside but then left the shopping centre with Mithat Lleshi and they were not seen on CCTV again.

Mithat Lleshi was an Albanian asylum seeker and the six men involved in the fight were also thought to have been Albanian although they were never caught. It was reported in August 2005 that three of the men had been arrested in Albania and that it was thought that they might go on trial there. There was no extradition treaty with Albania. However, in August 2017 his death was still being reported as unsolved.

It was said that they had been identified from CCTV footage with help from the Asylum Support Team as well as the Albanian Immigration Service, the community, an appeal on the Crimewatch television program and through Albanian forums and functions.

The Northampton bus station has now been demolished.

Ouahid Chakib

Age: 49

Sex: male

Date: 7 Jul 2001

Place: London

The death of Ouahid Chakib was reported as undetected by the Metropolitan Police in a Freedom of Information request.

No further information is known.

John Holland

Age: unknown

Sex: male

Date: 4 Jul 2001

Place: Hansom Close, West Drayton, Middlesex

John Holland was stabbed in the communal corridor of his flat in West Drayton.

A neighbour was tried for his murder but acquitted.

John Holland had been at a neighbour's flat in West Drayton waiting for a delivery of heroin and when it arrived he went back to his own flat.

A while later a commotion was heard in the communal corridor at the flats and when some people went out to see they saw the neighbour standing over John Holland who was bleeding heavily with a stab wound to his stomach.

John Holland was taken to hospital but died the following day.

At first the neighbour said that someone else had stabbed him but later admitted that he was responsible saying that he had not meant to stab him.

The judge told the jury that it was impossible for anyone other than the neighbour to know what had happened in the flat.

The jury retired for about two hours and cleared the man of both murder and manslaughter.

Mohammed Warsame

Age: 20

Sex: male

Date: 21 Jun 2001

Place: London

The death of Mohammed Warsame was declared undetected by the Metropolitan Police in a Freedom of Information request.

He was Afro-Caribbean.

No further information is known.

Alec Christopher

Age: 62

Sex: male

Date: 20 Jun 2001

Place: Avenue Road, Southall

Alec Christopher was stabbed as he walked along Avenue Road in Southall at 6.50am on 20 June 2001.

He was found in the road near the junction of Avenue Road and Cambridge Road with a single stab wound and taken to hospital where he died later that day.

The police said that there was a connection between his murder and an attack on another man some time earlier when a man had been stabbed in the head. They said that they had also interviewed several Somalian men that had been seen in Southall Park about 25 minutes earlier. There was said to have been a common link between Alec Christopher and the other man, that being the occupier of the house where the Somalian men had been drinking all night and where they regularly drank.

The police said that they had interviewed four of the five Somalian men but were still trying to find the fifth Somalian man who they described as aged between 30 and 40 years old, between 5ft 8ins and 5ft 10ins tall and with black balding hair, a black moustache, a goatee and with a slim build.

A CCTV camera recorded Alec Christopher around the time he was stabbed. It was thought that the footage caught him shortly after he had been stabbed and showed him rubbing and dabbing his hands.

He was later found to have had defensive injuries on his hands.

A CCTV camera had also recorded a woman walking along the street in the same direction as Alec Christopher and it was thought that she might be able to provide some fresh intelligence or have even talked to Alec Christopher. She was said to have been aged about 40 to 50 years old.

Jody Burns

Age: 27

Sex: male

Date: 15 Jun 2001

Place: High St, Runcorn, Cheshire

Jody Burns was killed in a street fight involving up to 60 people at a taxi rank on the High Street in the Old Town in Runcorn.

He had been out in the High Street on 15 June 2001 when he got involved in a string of fights between 12.30am and 1.30am.

Jody Burns was taken to hospital after being injured but died later that day. He had suffered from serious head injuries.

He was seen on CCTV trying to break up a fight outside the Bank Chambers pub shortly before but when the fighting spread to the taxi rank he was injured.

It was said that the disturbance in general had been going on for about 45 minutes before the police arrived.

Colin Beer

Age: 42

Sex: male

Date: 14 Jun 2001

Place: North Hill, Plymouth

Colin Beer died after being punched.

It was thought that he had been involved in an incident of road rage.

He had been out drinking at the Hyde Park pub in the Mutley district on Saturday 9 June 2001 and was seen walking along Mutley Plain, through the traffic, up to North Hill. It was thought that at some point he had become involved in an incident and a driver had got out of their car and punched him.

Colin Beer fell to the ground and suffered from a fractured skull after hitting his head. He died 5 days later in Derriford Hospital, Plymouth on 14 June 2001.

He had left the Hyde Park pub at 6pm and was seen walking in and out of traffic. He was seen to make contact with a wing mirror of a blue Peugeot 406 car, either hitting it or bumping into it. Witnesses then saw a man get out of a red Vauxhall Cavalier car at 6.15pm and hit Colin Beer. The car was said to have had an eight-inch black sticker on the offside of the boot. The driver was described as being aged around 30 years old, of a medium build, with a thin-face, short brown hair and a goatee beard. He was said to have been wearing a white shirt and blue or black jeans.

Colin Beer had lived in Devonport.

John Dickinson

Age: 35

Sex: male

Date: 11 Jun 2001

Place: London

The death of John Dickinson was reported as undetected by the Metropolitan Police in a Freedom of Information request.

No other information is known.

Christopher Hewitt

Age: 18

Sex: male

Date: 10 Jun 2001

Place: Jolly Roger Pub, All Hallows Road, Bristol

Christopher Hewitt was stabbed in a brawl outside the Jolly Roger pub in All Hallows Road.

He was stabbed 10 times. Fifteen people had been sitting on a wall close by but were reluctant to speak to the police. There were also said to have been a lot of people inside the pub that might have seen something who also appeared reluctant to speak to the police.

Christopher Hewitt was from Jamaica and had been visiting the UK and Bristol for a few weeks.

It was thought that some Yardies from East Kingston, in Jamaica, had gone to the Jolly Roger pub on the night and had sent message in to Christopher Hewitt to come outside. When he did he was slashed 24 times with knives and stabbed. His stomach was ripped open and he had been stabbed through the skull.

Police later found a sheath knife nearby which they said had been one of the murder weapons. The police also found a strip of metal from a carving knife 7 to 8ins long which was thought to have been another weapon used.

During their investigation, 19 people were arrested but no one was ever charged, and little evidence could be found.

Following his death, the police launched Operation Atrium to target drug related crime and in six weeks managed to arrest 85 people. They also recovered over £30,000 worth of heroin, £18,500 in cash, a Webley self-loading automatic pistol, several replica guns and some shotgun cartridges. They said that hundreds of people were flying into the UK from Jamaica carrying drugs, often internally at a risk to their lives resulting in about 90kg of cocaine arriving each week,

9kgs of which the police said was arriving in Bristol.

Jacey Frederick Valentine John Charles

Age: 23

Sex: male

Date: 9 Jun 2001

Place: Drummonds Nightclub, Marsh Wall, Isle of Dogs

Jacey Charles was stabbed to death outside the Drummonds nightclub in Marsh Wall.

He had got involved in an argument outside the club and was approached by four men. The argument then became violent and he was stabbed.

He was taken to the Royal London Hospital but soon died.

The police later spoke to about 75% of the people that had been at the club and four men were later arrested but no one was charged.

He was an IT consultant.

Donovan Williams

Age: 24

Sex: male

Date: 7 Jun 2001

Place: Barrow Road, Streatham

Donovan Williams was shot in Barrow Road, Streatham on 7 June 2001.

No other information is known.

Sami Mustafa and Hasan Mamali

Age: 26 and 23

Sex: male and male

Date: 27 May 2001

Place: Islington

Sami Mustafa and Hasan Mamali were shot dead in Islington.

They had been sitting in a BMW convertible car in Islington at the time.

Hasan Mamali was hit in the back of his head in the car whilst Sami Mustafa was hit in the back, chest and skull after he got of the car and tried to run off.

It was thought that they had been involved in the Turkish drugs trade and that they had crossed people involved in the local criminal underworld.

Richard Rayner

Age: 43

Sex: male

Date: 25 May 2001

Place: River Bank Cafe, Stratford

Richard Rayner was shot in the head.

He had been waiting for breakfast at the River Bank cafe in the East End when a man on a motorbike drove up and shot him in the head.

He was a plumber and it was thought that his shooting was a case of mistaken identity.

It was said that a prime suspect that was living in Spain was alerted to the fact that the police were planning to interview him over the murder.

Billy Webb

Age: 42

Sex: male

Date: 24 May 2001

Place: Whiteledge Road, Bryn, Ashton-in-Makerfield

Billy Webb was shot dead as he slept in bed.

He was a big-time drug dealer and had been out earlier in the night in Hindley with his girlfriend after which they had got home at 3am on 24 May 2001. He was then shot twice in the head when two gunmen burst into his bedroom. His girlfriend who was sleeping with him was also seriously injured.

The gunman had had a key to his home and had let themselves in.

Initially the police said they were looking for three black men that had been seen near the flat twice the day before driving a white or powder blue Ford Mondeo or Orion car.

The police said that they were also trying to trace a motorcyclist that was seen nearby.

However, in 2003 two other men were tried for conspiracy to murder in relation to his murder. It was not suggested that they were the gunmen but there was insufficient evidence and the judge instructed the jury to find them not guilty.

Two and a half years earlier in August 1997 Billy Webb had been having a meeting with another drug dealer in the Ancient Shepherd pub and were later walking along Bankfield Street in Bolton when Dillon Hull, a 5-year-old boy and the son of the other drug dealer, was shot in the head. A man wearing a crash helmet had leapt out of the shadows and fired four shots, one which hit Dillon Hull in the head, another hitting the man and two missing. The man survived, and the gunman was later convicted for Dillon Hull's murder. It was said that he had been paid between £5,000 and £10,000 to shoot the man that Billy Webb was meeting after Billy Webb and the man had fallen out. At the time Billy Webb was described as a gangland drug boss. The man who shot the drug dealers son, Dillon Hull, was convicted in 1998 for the murder of Dillon Hull and sentenced to

25 years. When he was shot, Dillon Hull had been walking hand in hand with his father.

It was said that Billy Webb and another man had been operating a heroin and cocaine smuggling business together. They were said to have run a multi-million-pound drugs empire from a small cafe, Debbie's Diner, and to have ruled over the local underworld with an iron fist. The man on trial was said to have been the brains of the operation whilst Billy Webb was said to have been the brawn. It was said that they paid their employees a salary and had regular director's meetings. The police said that they were unable to get any of the smaller drug dealers to talk because they were scared of Billy Webb and his partner and had seen people attacked with baseball bats, hit on the head with a hammer and also seen their girlfriends raped. The police then started to record the meetings at the cafe and after an 18-month operation they arrested Billy Webb and his partner.

Billy Webb and the man were due to stand trial together, but Billy Webb was shot before he could attend court. Also, the man on trial, Billy Webb's alleged business partner in the drugs cartel fled the country during the trial after a Christmas break in

2001. Ten other members of the gang were convicted for 77-years in total whilst Billy Webb's partner was sentenced to 22-years in his absence. He was later extradited in 2004 but refused to answer any questions regarding Billy Webb's murder.

Mary Hancock

Age: 92

Sex: female

Date: 18 May 2001

Place: Leyland Road, Southport

Mary Hancock died after being mugged.

She was mugged on 19 April 2001 at 2.40pm and had her handbag stolen. She suffered from a broken pelvis, cuts and bruises and died four weeks later on 18 May 2001.

She was thrown to the ground during the attack after a white saloon car, driven by a man, pulled up and a woman got out, pulled her handbag from her, and then got back into the car which then drove off.

After the mugging she was left lying on the pavement.

It was said that she had just £10 in her handbag.

Andre Jan Aylward

Age: 27

Sex: male

Date: 12 May 2001

Place: Valleyfield Road, Streatham Common North

Andre Aylward was shot in his car.

He had been driving his black 5-series BMW, which had blacked out windows, along Valleyfield Road at about 2.10am on 12 May 2001 when six shots were fired from a handgun at his car. After the shooting, he lost control of his car and crashed into some parked cars and a garden.

He had been hit twice in the head and neck and was taken to King's College Hospital where he died around 4am.

A few minutes before the shooting a grey 7 series BMW car was seen alongside his and the police said that they were seeking to identify it. It was thought that the car had just previously been at a nearby BP petrol station at the top of Knights Hill, where it had bought some petrol.

It was thought that the attack might have been a case of road rage or mistaken identity.

He lived nearby in Streatham and was thought to have driven home from a friend's house where he had been, along Crown Lane and Streatham Common North to the junction with Leigham Court Road and then along Valleyfield Road.

The police said that they found nothing in his background to suggest that he had been involved in any criminal activity. They said that they thought that the reason for his murder was based on the events shortly before the shooting rather than any long running events or targetted gangland activity as it would not have been readily predictable that he would have been driving in that area at that time.

He was a pet shop manager at Oliver's Pet Supplies in Streatham Vale, and a car enthusiast. His BMW car had tinted windows, a lowered suspension and a loud car stereo.

Steven Daniel Richard McCalla

Age: 26

Sex: male

Date: 10 May 2001

Place: Brixton, South London

Steven McCalla was shot as he sat in a car in Brixton.

He had been driving his convertible VW Golf car with his girlfriend sat in the front passenger seat when a red Fiat car pulled up behind them and flashed its lights.

Then a person in the red Fiat car fired five shots through the VW Golf car's driver's window hitting Steven McCalla three times and his girlfriend once in the arm.

Hilda Lockert

Age: 84

Sex: female

Date: 30 Apr 2001

Place: Myatts Field Estate, Stockwell, South London

Hilda Lockert died after being mugged.

She lived on the Myatts Field Estate in Stockwell.

She was thrown down some stairs and was taken to hospital with a broken left leg and a metal plate was inserted. However, she died a while later from a blood clot.

She had been mugged six times before and had given up reporting the attacks to the police as no one was ever caught.

Her attacker took £15 in cash, a bus pass and a Tesco loyalty card.

It was said that her two attackers were no older than 15 years old and were said to have been black.

Her neighbour said that Hilda Lockert had once told her in conversation that the youths on the estate would end up killing someone and noted that she could not have known that it would have been her.

She died on her 86th birthday.

Corey Wright and Wayne Henry

Age: 20 and 19

Sex: male and male

Date: 21 Apr 2001

Place: Lower Clapton

Corey Wright and Wayne Henry were shot in a car in Lower Clapton.

They had just left the Chimes nightclub in their blue BMW convertible car when they were both shot.

After the shooting, the driver lost control of the BMW convertible car and it ran into three women and then crashed into a night bus.

Corey Wright was one of six youths convicted for conspiracy to commit grievous bodily harm with intent in relation to the murder of 16-year-old Kingsley Iyasara whose murder is still also technically unsolved. Of the six youths, Menelik Robinson was also later murdered in 2000, and his murder is also unsolved. Kingsley Iyasara was beaten and shot dead in February 1997 in Carlton Lodge Estate, Finsbury Park in north London by what was described as sixteen youths armed with sticks and bats.

Rebecca Hall

Age: 19

Sex: female

Date: 13 Apr 2001

Place: Thornton Street, Bradford

Rebecca Hall was found dead in an alleyway.

She was a prostitute and had worked around the Bradford area. She disappeared on 13 April 2001 and was later found dead in the alleyway on 26 April 2001 having been beaten to death.

She had been stripped and then beaten to death. Her cause of death was given as head injuries. When she was attacked her clothes were ripped off of her.

She was last seen when she left her flat at Lydford House, in Elizabeth Street, Little Horton, at about 10pm on 13 April 2001. It was thought that she had been heading off towards Thornton Road when she left.

When her body was found she was naked.

Rebecca Hall had been a heroin addict and had a four-month-old baby boy.

She was 5ft 5ins tall, slim, and had dyed red hair cut in a bob-style. She had been wearing black leggings and a purple sheer top with knee-length black boots and had had a Motorola Star Tac mobile phone and a distinctive limited edition watch with a South Park cartoon character. The phone and watch were never found.

It was thought that her killer had known her or had been a regular customer. It was also thought that her killer was local to the area.

In 2008, police re-examined DNA samples from her strap top and knickers after improvements in DNA examination meant that samples which were previously too small to analyse could reveal more.

In January 2019 a woman was arrested on suspicion of her murder.

David George Roads

Age: 55

Sex: male

Date: 10 Apr 2001

Place: Cowper Road, Kingston

David George Roads was shot in an alleyway as he walked back to Latchmere House prison where he was an inmate.

He was shot twice in the head at close range, both bullets being fired before he hit the ground.

The police said that it was a well-planned attack.

He was last seen on the Monday by his wife at 4.30pm in Bromley, south London and later spoke to his son on his mobile phone at 9.51pm in Park Road, Richmond. He was found dead at 10.20pm that night in an alleyway off Cowper Road and Sopwith Close.

David Roads had been convicted for possessing industrial semtex, firearms and ecstasy in March 1997 and sentenced to 10 years. He had also been on a charge of conspiring to commit murder but was acquitted. He was said to have been a quartermaster, supplying guns, and was alleged to have supplied guns to a man involved with the IRA and the Irish National Liberation Army who was later convicted of attempted murder.

He had been on a special programme to re-integrate him into society and had been working for a glazing firm in London in October 2000 and had been on his way back to Latchmere House prison for a 10pm curfew.

Mehmet Selimoglu

Age: 33

Sex: male

Date: 10 Apr 2001

Place: London

The death of Mehmet Selimoglu was detailed as undetected in a Metropolitan Police Freedom of Information Request.

He was white.

No further information is known.

Florence Ansell

Age: 90

Sex: female

Date: 3 Apr 2001

Place: Blakesware Gardens, Enfield, North London

Florence Ansell was beaten to death.

A man was charged but was cleared because there were no witnesses.

She had been punched in the face and then dragged to the ground on 14 March 2001 and then left lying in the street. she was taken to hospital where she died 20 days later on Tuesday 3 April 2001.

Her attacker got away with £30.

Florence Ansell suffered from fractures to hcr shoulder and pelvis which later caused deep vein thrombosis to flare up resulting in her death.

The man that was tried, who was said to have been a heroin addict and to have robbed her for money for drugs, was arrested after it was said that he had told a friend that he had 'robbed an old granny'. However, it was heard in court that the friend was an unreliable witness and that there was otherwise insufficient evidence to link the man to Florence Ansell's death.

Mark Thompson and George Price

Age: 30 and 34

Sex: male and male

Date: 2 Apr 2001

Place: Ince Blundell, Crosby

Mark Thompson and George Price were found shot dead in a field in Ince Blundell.

They had been beaten, stabbed and shot. An attempt had also been made to set their bodies on fire with petrol.

They had both been shot once each in the head. It was thought that George Price might have already been dead from stab wounds when he was shot but that Mark Thompson might have been killed by the shot to the head.

They were both found dead the following morning.

It was thought that they were last seen by a wooded copse near the M57 in Huyton at 7pm when a person saw three men near the wood carrying a large shooting target.

The last confirmed sighting of them was in a maroon Vauxhall Astra estate car with registration number S921 ORN as the car drove from Newark Close into Knowsley Lane in Huyton. The wooded copse was opposite Knowsley Lane.

The copse was thought to have been used as a practice range and a .25 calibre bullet found embedded in a tree there was later matched to the calibre of a bullet found in Mark Thompson's body. The bullet that killed George Price had gone straight through his head and was not found.

It was also thought that they might have been in the woods themselves an hour before they died, firing guns. The witness that said they saw three men near the wood said that the large target they were carrying was a full-sized target of a soldier and that one of them had had an army-style gun. Marks were found on a number of trees in the wood indicating that someone had removed bullets from them, but one tree was found with the bullet remaining in it.

A person said that Mark Thompson and George Price had both been seen with guns a few days before their murders and that they would often fire them in makeshift gun alleys around Huyton.

The gun was thought to have been a pocket-sized gun popular with American women and often called a handbag gun. The gun was said to have been similar to the one that had been used to kill Warren Selkirk, a drugs courier, in Crosby Marina in 1999 as well as Jill Dando in London, also in 1999.

Corey Brown

Age: 22

Sex: male

Date: 2 Apr 2001

Place: Forest Gate, London

Corey Brown was shot whilst driving his car in Forest Gate.

He was shot with an automatic gun and hit ten times.

Stuart Lubbock

Age: 31

Sex: male

Date: 31 Mar 2001

Place: Royston, Essex

Stuart Lubbock was found dead in a swimming pool after having been sexually assaulted.

He had been at a party at the house of a famous celebrity in Royston, Essex, where he had taken drugs including Ecstasy and cocaine. He was also said to have been three times over the legal drink and drive limit.

It was said that before his death he had been seriously sexually assaulted and would have been in excruciating pain afterwards and have had trouble walking. It was noted that he might have been forcibly held down whilst the sexual assault took place. He was said to have had anal injuries and it was said that it was not thought that his injuries were the result of a consensual sexual act. The pathologist that carried out his post-mortem said that Stuart Lubbock had extensive internal bruising, lacerations and inflammation and that his injuries would have been caused within a few hours of his death. His comments at the time read 'cause of death emersion subject to toxicology' and 'deceased has been buggered w/I [within] last few hours, obvious tearing visible'.

It was initially thought that Stuart Lubbock had drowned. It was also suggested that he might have died from asphyxiation or cardiac arrest occurring during the non-consensual sexual act, and serious sexual assault. One pathologist said that Stuart Lubbock had been alive when he had gone into the water and that the cocaine in his system might have caused him to inhale water but that he might not have been able to clear it. However, another pathologist said that he could not rule out the possibility that Stuart Lubbock had been already dead when he had entered the water. An independent pathologist said that when he examined Stuart Lubbock's body he could find none of the typical signs of drowning and concluded that his death was unascertained.

Later police findings stated that the police thought that his death by drowning had been staged.

When Stuart Lubbock was found floating in the pool he was pulled out and attempts were made to resuscitate him. At the inquest, the pathologist was asked if his internal injuries could have been caused whilst he was being resuscitated and the pathologist said 'No. Absolutely not.'.

Another pathologist said that he found small haemorrhages in Stuart Lubbock's facial blood vessels which indicated that he might have been squeezed around the neck at some stage and could have been caused during some form of erotic asphyxiation.

Stuart Lubbock had been a factory supervisor and had been married with two children but was divorced. He had met the famous celebrity at the Millennium nightclub in Harlow, Essex, on the night of 30 March 2001, the night he died, and had gone back to the famous celebrity's bungalow in Roydon afterwards at 2.35am with a group of other people. Stuart Lubbock had been at the Millennium nightclub with his brother where they met the famous celebrity who was with his friend. The famous celebrity then later invited Stuart Lubbock, and some other people, back to his bungalow. There were a total of nine people at the bungalow.

Whilst at the bungalow, a witness said that several people stripped off and got into a Jacuzzi along with Stuart Lubbock who was then seen to get out and jump into the swimming pool, laughing and joking. He was then later found floating in it unconscious. However, the witnesses statement was later thought to have been possibly false.

An ambulance was later called at 5.48am on 31 March 2001. The ambulance arrived at 5.56am and found Stuart Lubbock unconscious by the side of the pool. He was then taken to the Princess Alexander Hospital in Harlow where he was treated and later died at 8.23am. It was noted at the time by the ambulance crew that when they found Stuart Lubbock it was thought that he was already clinically dead.

After the ambulance had arrived they called the police at 5.51am to notify them and some policemen arrived at the bungalow around 6am.

Later that afternoon the cause of death was given as immersion and it was noted that Stuart Lubbock had serious injuries to his anus.

It was noted that at the time the ambulance arrived that there was no immediate reason to suspect the possibility of murder and that his injuries looked like the results of drowning. This note was said to be significant because of later claims that the police had not sealed off the bungalow and its grounds properly as part of a murder crime scene. It was only later after Stuart Lubbock died and his post-mortem was carried out that his anal injuries were noticed, by which time the guests at the party had cleaned up and the famous celebrity had locked up the premises.

The famous celebrity, who was openly gay at the time, was a TV presenter and worked for a major company earning what was described as the highest salary of all TV presenters in the United Kingdom at the time.

After Stuart Lubbock was taken away the police gave the famous celebrity a caution for the possession of cannabis and for allowing his home to be used for the smoking of cannabis.

Stuart Lubbock's inquest took place on 10 September 2002 and on 13 September 2002 the jury returned an open verdict.

In November 2002 the famous celebrity demanded that the Essex Police re-investigate the matters surrounding Stuart Lubbock's death, claiming that he did not believe that his internal injuries could have been inflicted at his bungalow and said that he thought that they happened when he was at the mortuary. He claimed that after Stuart Lubbock's body was taken to the Princess Alexandra Hospital in Harlow at 8.20am there had been an eight-hour gap between him arriving and being examined and noted that the pathologist that had examined him at 4pm had said that Stuart Lubbock's internal injuries were four hours old. He claimed that there was a discrepancy there and the famous celebrity said that he wanted to prove that the anal injuries could not have happened at his house.

It was also noted that in 2006 the famous celebrity had given an interview to GQ magazine, a famous magazine, in which he had been asked whether he knew of anyone that was hiding secrets about Stuart Lubbock's death in which the famous celebrity had replied 'Yes. But I'm not going to say their names. I just hope they are brave enough to come forward one day.'.

It was also noted that in 2006 one of the other people at the party had given an interview to a reporter of the News Of The World which led the Essex Police to open an investigation regarding whether that person had committed perjury at the inquest.

In the 2007 IPCC report it was stated that some of the witnesses at the party had given conflicting accounts of what had happened. The report stated that the police thought that Stuart Lubbock died outside of the swimming pool and that he did not swim in the pool as was claimed by some of the people at the party and that his drowning was staged.

On 14 June 2007, the Essex Police arrested the famous celebrity and two other men on suspicion of the murder of Stuart Lubbock and serious sexual assault after it was found that tapes had been seized from the famous celebrity's literary agent that detailed conversations that the famous celebrity had had with other people. The famous celebrity was held for questioning and the police were given permission to hold him for another 12 hours and he was released the next day on bail. When the famous celebrity later answered bail on 31 July 2007 he was held again for questioning for 12 hours after which he was released and told that no charges would be made.

In a statement the Essex Police said, 'The judgement is clear that the officers leading the investigation into Stuart Lubbock's death had reasonable grounds to suspect that the famous celebrity had raped or murdered Mr Lubbock at his home address and had reasonable grounds for believing that it was necessary to arrest him.'. However, they also noted that the threshold for forming that suspicion was low and fell far short of that required to charge or convict a person.

It was also noted that in 2009, some items of evidence had gone missing from the crime scene, including a pool thermometer and a door handle which were thought might have been used to carry out the sexual assault on Stuart Lubbock. It was stated that the thermometer and the door handle were photographed at the scene but that they were not removed for examination.

Stuart Lubbock's father later complained that at the time Stuart Lubbock's body was found, the people at the party were not taken away from the house and that some of them were allowed to stay behind and tidy up resulting in certain items possibly not being found or forensically examined. He also noted that blood found on boxer shorts, towels and a robe was not promptly investigated and that the police investigation was suspended prematurely. He said that there were a catalogue of errors in the police investigation and that he was sure that if the police had done their job properly then he was sure that there would have been people charged.

The IPCC 2007 report stated that a policeman stood guard at the bungalow at 6.20am as the ambulance took Stuart Lubbock away and that afterwards they searched the grounds to see who was there and that during the course of the morning they took statements from everybody. It was noted that at the time the famous celebrity had gone to a flat nearby and had instructed a friend to tell all the people at the party to tell the police that he had not been at the bungalow that night or at the time Stuart Lubbock had been found unconscious, and as was alleged, in the swimming pool.

However, the famous celebrity was soon found at a nearby flat where he had gone and brought back and questioned and it was noted that both he and his friend were still under the influence of alcohol.

The report also stated that the police had put everyone still at the bungalow into separate rooms for questioning and had informed the famous celebrity that Stuart Lubbock had died, shortly after he died at 8.23am.

It was also noted that people had been seen cleaning things up around the house at various times and were asked not to.

The report stated that at 9.45am a policeman arrived at the bungalow to take photos and that he took a photo of what was thought to have been a floating thermometer which consisted of a rod approximately four or five inches long and half an inch wide which protruded from a thick rounded rubber or plastic end that was about three inches in diameter. It was noted later that the item was not collected as evidence. The photographer also took a photo of some blood on the patio by the swimming pool. He said at the time that he remembered impressing on one of the men at the party not to touch anything.

Items taken as evidence included some clothing, wet shorts, two bloodstained towels, a towelling robe and a baseball cap that was found at the bottom of the pool. The police also took some suspected drug paraphernalia.

The report also noted that when the Deputy Chief Constable of Essex Police was called and informed about the situation at 9.55am that morning he had said 'this is a high-profile incident and that's why I want the MIT (Major Investigation Team) involved'.

The house was sealed up at 12.20pm on 31 March, with a policeman on guard outside, but one of the guests returned at 12.30pm on behalf of the police to take the temperature of the pool, but didn't leave until 2.10pm, during which time he was in the property unaccompanied.

Later on 1 April 2001 the police went back to the scene and took other items including the glass that was in the photograph as well as the contents of the outside dustbin. Later that same day it was determined that the examination of the scene was complete, and the property was released back to a representative of the famous celebrity.

The 2007 IPCC report noted that the Murder Investigation Manual 2000 published by the National Crime Faculty and Association of Chief Police Officers, Crime Committee stated that 'The initial information that an offence has been committed may be of a precise or imprecise nature' and that 'where death or serious injury or where circumstances appear suspicious THINK MURDER, crime scenes are precious, opportunities to harvest evidence should not be wasted' and further advised that ' If in doubt investigate as a murder until the evidence proves otherwise'. The report looked into whether the policeman in charge at the scene of the crime that morning had done his job properly. It was heard that he said he did not think that the incident was suspicious and was never asked if it was suspicious. The report stated that things that should have been apparent to him included:

- Stuart Lubbock was in resuscitation, but it was very likely that he would die.
- his identity was unknown.
- his history was unknown.
- it was not known how he got into the swimming pool.
- there were allegations that certain witnesses allegedly withheld the fact

that the famous celebrity had been present and had left the scene.
- initial accounts given by witnesses contained inconsistencies in respect of key points.
- suspected blood was present on items at the side of the pool.
- suspected blood was present on the patio by the side of the pool.
- there was broken glass by the side of the pool.
- there was evidence of a party and some witnesses appeared to be under the influence of alcohol.
- the possible use of drugs could not be discounted.

As such, the report concluded that the policeman in charge, an inspector, should have concluded that the situation was suspicious and that if he had done so and had followed the protocol as laid out by the Essex Police policy dealing with 'Homicides and all Unnatural Deaths' and effectively preserved the scene it was possible that the door handle and thermometer, which were not collected might have been recovered by a policeman. The report concluded that the complaint against the policeman was upheld, stating that he had failed to carry out his duties conscientiously and diligently as required by paragraph 5 of the police Code of Conduct.

The 2007 IPCC report also noted that a complaint that the blood on the towels and scrapings from the side of the pool were not tested forensically were upheld. It was said that Stuart Lubbock's boxer shorts, a robe and two towels were taken in evidence along with scrapings from by the pool that were thought to have been blood and that semen was found on the boxer shorts and robe but only the semen on the robe was tested and was found to have not been Stuart Lubbock's, but that of another identified person. However, it was found that testing of the blood and semen on the boxer shorts was not carried out, and nor was testing on the blood of the two towels. The blood on the robe and two towels was not tested until 2007. The scrapings were also tested in 2007 and determined not to have been blood. It was noted that between 1 April 2001 and 30 August 2001, a total of 98 items were submitted to the FSS laboratory for various tests, most of which were completed successfully, with results obtained, including items such as hairs, fibres, sweepings, swabs, clothing, glasses, bottles, household items and tools, and as such it was concluded that it was probable that the police had asked for the boxer shorts, robe and towels to be examined but that they had not been done. It was also noted that some of the work had been designated as urgent and as such the report states that it was difficult to understand why the blood on the towels, robe, boxer shorts and scrapings from the patio were not profiled earlier. As such, the 2007 IPCC report upheld Stuart Lubbock's father's complaint that the police had failed to analyse the items and as such constituted a failure by the Chief Superintendent to carry out his duties conscientiously and diligently as required by paragraph 5 of the police Code of Conduct.

A further complaint against the Essex Police was also upheld by the 2007 IPCC report regarding the decision to close the investigation into Stuart Lubbock's death prematurely. It was noted that the investigation into his death was suspended on 11 December 2001. The Chief Superintendent wrote in his policy book 'As a result of the medical experts' meeting it would appear that there is no medical evidence available to us which establishes any causal link between any person and Stuart Lubbock's death. It is therefore not in the public interest to continue to pursue an investigation into his death. A file will be prepared for the CPS to consider if the evidence available could support a charge against any person. HM Coroner has been briefed and wished the file to be submitted to the CPS before coming to her.'. The report noted that Chapter 12.2 of the Murder Investigation Manual 2000 stated: 'Current situation reports (formally known as closing reports) should be completed in respect of investigations into all undetected offences of murder, attempted murder, stranger rapes and any other investigation into a serious offence for example abduction' and that while the police were not investigating a clear offence of murder, it could not be completely discounted, nor could the possibility that Stuart Lubbock was the victim of a rape. When the Chief Superintendent was questioned he said that he thought that all lines of enquiry were closed and that there was no link between Stuart Lubbock's anal injuries and his death. However, the report stated that all lines of enquiry were not finished as there were still outstanding forensic results. The Chief Superintendent also said that he thought that it was no longer in the public interest to continue the investigation. The report concluded that it appeared that the Chief Superintendent had suspended the investigation mainly in the light of the medical evidence that stated that there was no link between Stuart Lubbock's anal injuries and his death. However, it further stated that there were three medical opinions, that he had drowned after consuming drink and drugs, that he might have asphyxiated or the third opinion that he might have suffered a heart attack resulting from his anal injuries. Again, it was found that the decision not to continue to pursue (suspend) the investigation into Stuart Lubbock's death without taking into account outstanding enquiries and without recording a rationale for not completing these amounted to a failure by the Chief Superintendent to carry out his duties conscientiously and diligently as required by paragraph 5 of the police Code of Conduct.

The famous celebrity later sued the Essex Police for wrongful arrest in July 2015 and on 18 August 2017 the famous celebrity was told by the High Court in London that he was entitled to more than nominal damages for the wrongful arrest although no value for the claim was made by the judges, but it was noted that the famous celebrity had valued his claim at more that £2,400,000. He said that his career had been destroyed by the arrest. The police had said that the famous celebrity was only entitled to nominal compensation after it was determined that the policeman that had arrested him did not have reasonable enough grounds to suspect that the famous celebrity was guilty.

Herbert Schwarz

Age: 74

Sex: male

Date: 27 Mar 2001

Place: London

The death of Herbert Schwarz was detailed as undetected in a Metropolitan Police Freedom of Information Request.

He was white.

No further information is known.

David Williamson

Age: 58

Sex: male

Date: 26 Mar 2001

Place: Sutton-on-the-Forest, North Yorkshire

David Williamson was found unconscious in a lay-by by a footpath and later died.

A man was tried for his murder in 2002 but acquitted.

The layby which was on the Huby to Sutton-on-the-Forest road, north of York, was half a mile from his home in Milton House, Sutton-on-the-Forest.

He had a fractured skull and was taken to the Leeds General Infirmary where he later died without regaining consciousness.

It was said that he had gone along the footpath, which was a shortcut through the edge of a small wood at about 11.30pm on the previous Sunday night, 25 March 2017 after leaving a party that had been held at the nearby Star Inn in Huby. He was found at 5.30am the following morning, 26 March 2017.

The man that was tried for his murder was said to have made a confession whilst on a charge for burglary, but the judge ruled that his confession was inadmissible. It was said that he had given his confession whilst in a police cell during which it would have been required for a certain document to be completed and signed before any cell interview took place, however, the document was signed after the cell interview. The judge said that the document should have been signed before the interview and the interview should have been formally taped. The judge noted that there was no suggestion that there was any bad faith existing on behalf of the policemen in what they were seeking to do noting that they had been concerned at the time that if they had not continued talking to the man that he might have not gone ahead with his confession and then clammed up. The judge noted that although other taped interviews had been made, he did not think that the man would get a fair trial and noted that there was also no other corroborating evidence in the case. It was also noted that some parts of his confession did not fit the facts. In his confession he had said that he had dragged David Williamson along the street, but it was heard that the pathologist said that David Williamson's injuries did not support that assertion. It was also heard that the man had told police where he had buried an iron bar that he had used in the attack but that when the police went with him to find it, no iron bar could be found. The judge also noted that a defence psychiatrist had been told by the man that he had only confessed to get respect from the police so they didn't think he was a dickhead.

Ian Michael Dowling

Age: 39

Sex: male

Date: 15 Mar 2001

Place: Sidney Street, Grantham

Ian Michael Dowling was found shot dead in his home.

He was shot in the heart and lungs after going to the door to answer a knock. After being shot he was able to stumble into his kitchen and died later that evening.

Three people were tried for his murder. Two of them were acquitted whilst a third man, his best friend, was convicted of conspiracy to murder but had his conviction later quashed after it was heard that the police had used illegal surveillance and as such, the conviction was unsafe. It was said that the police had illegally recorded conversations that the man had had with his solicitor in the exercise yard at Sleaford police station.

It was said that Ian Dowling had been seeing another man's wife, a 36-year-old school dinner lady, and that she had told her husband, the man that was convicted of conspiracy to murder, by a text message via her phone, that their 13-year marriage was over and that the man had then conspired to murder Ian Dowling by hiring a man to shoot him. He was said to have orchestrated the killing with underworld criminals.

The school dinner lady left her husband and went to live with Ian Dowling at a house on Sidney Street and that she took their three children with her.

The court heard that Ian Dowling and the man convicted of conspiracy to murder had exchanged heated text messages via their telephones whilst trying to vie for the affections of Ian Dowling's wife beforehand.

The husband admitted that he had taken part in a conspiracy to assault Ian Dowling in early 2001 but said that he had called it off. He said that he thought that Ian Dowling had been shot by criminal contacts of his, and that his shooting was related to drugs.

Baby

Age: 0

Sex: male

Date: 11 Mar 2001

Place: Harewood Drive, Edinburgh

The body of a newly born child was found beside a footpath, between Harewood Drive and Harewood Road, in the Craigmillar area of Edinburgh at about 8am on 11 March 2001.

It was burned and mutilated.

The child had been wearing a multi-coloured suit made from cotton that depicted various Disney characters including Mickey Mouse, Donald Duck and Pluto on a white background with red dots. It was said that the item was not sold by The Disney Store or other retailers such as Marks & Spencer or Baby Gap and that it was thought that the item had been made by a small operation that was using the pattern and that it might have been sold at market stalls.

The child was also wrapped up in a blanket with a satin trim which had holes in it.

The police said that they were interested in hearing from anyone who remembered a woman being pregnant in the early part of 2001 and who did not go on to have the child.

The police said that they also found a label near where the child was found which was thought to have come from the sale of a china doll from The Leonardo Collection. They said that The Leonardo Collection manufactured about 100 different types of doll, but that they all had a porcelain face, arms and feet.

The police also found a bag from the interior design store Au Naturale near the child's body.

John Swain

Age: 42

Sex: male

Date: 16 Feb 2001

Place: London

The death of John Swain was detailed as undetected in a Metropolitan Police Freedom of Information Request.

He was white.

No further information is known.

Peter Beaumont Gowling

Age: 52

Sex: male

Date: 14 Feb 2001

Place: Osborne Road, Jesmond, Newcastle upon Tyne

Peter Beaumont Gowling was shot at his home in Jesmond.

He had answered the door when the doorbell rang during the afternoon on 14 February 2001 and was shot four times at point-blank range in the head and body.

His body was not found until midnight when his girlfriend got home and found him lying face down in the living room.

A neighbour said they heard a scream at 2pm and saw two men running away.

Peter Gowling had previously been convicted in 1997 for drug-money laundering and sentenced to 11 years.

Two men were seen running away from his home after the shooting and were caught on CCTV.

It was thought that his murder would have been related to him being caught with a large quantity of drugs which the police had taken and which, as such, had not realised profits to the drug dealers who had given him the drugs. It was said that Peter Gowling had refused to later pay for the drugs because he considered that he had paid his debt by imprisonment and that he might have been shot has a result. When he was shot he had only been out of prison for a short time.

Mark Connor

Age: 30

Sex: male

Date: 14 Feb 2001

Place: 16 Claire Court, Shoot Up Hill, Kilburn

Mark Connor was executed with a gunshot to the head at his flat in Claire Court, Shoot Up Hill, on Valentine's Day, 14 February 2001.

A man was tried for his murder at the Old Baily in 2001 but the case collapsed after the prosecution didn't produce enough evidence.

His body was found fully clothed in a bath full of water, shot in the back of the head, three days after he was last seen. He had also been beaten about the head and had six wounds to the back and side of it thought to have been caused by a blunt instrument such as the butt of a handgun. It was said that he had been put in the bath after he died.

His girlfriend, who lived at another one of Mark Connor's properties said that when she last saw him three days earlier he had left telling her that he had business to attend to and that she didn't see or hear from him again. She said that after she hadn't heard from him for a number of days she became worried and went round to his flat in Shoot Up Hill. They had been seeing each other for eight years after having met in Dublin.

His death was said to have been an execution style murder and that a pillow had been put to the back of his head which was then shot through. It was thought that he had been shot on 11 February 2001.

Mark Connor had three houses and was thought to have been involved in drug smuggling and tobacco importation as well as some kind of fraud. During the police operation it was found that Mark Connor, who was Irish, had previously lived in Dublin where he was described as the biggest drug dealer in west Dublin before he moved to London. It was said in 2012 that it was thought that he had been involved with a drug smuggler in Liverpool who was at that time serving 13 years for trafficking cocaine.

Shortly after Mark Connor was found dead it was found that his girlfriend, who found his body, had burnt some of his documents that related to the fraud he was involved with and had also walked off with two cheques for £17,500. Four days after finding Mark Connor's body she also admitted to the police that when she had gone to the flat she had gone with two other people and that they had tried to remove a bloodstained footprint from the carpet that one of the men had left. She said that she panicked and took a couple of letters and some birth certificates that Mark Connor had in false names which she then burned at another one of Mark Connor's properties in Shootup Hill.

She was convicted of perverting the course of justice but said that she had acted in panic and was given a conditional discharge.

She also said that she knew that Mark Connor had been involved in a scheme to smuggle cigarettes into the UK and that he had been told to raise £20,000 and to give it to a certain person but said that the cigarettes never materialised.

Mark Connor had also used a number of other names including Peter John Joyce,

Lawrence Ellis, Stitch, and Gerard Anthony Arbuckle.

The police later said that they believed the key to solving the mystery behind his murder lay in Dublin.

Francis Cross

Age: 19

Sex: male

Date: 9 Feb 2001

Place: Pulse Club, Liverpool

Francis Cross was shot outside the Pulse club in Liverpool.

He was shot in the early hours of a Sunday night.

His friend was also injured.

A man was questioned, but no further information is known.

Hussain Obad

Age: 19

Sex: male

Date: 7 Feb 2001

Place: Acorn Court, Acorn Housing Estate, Upper Warwick Street, Toxteth

Hussain Obad was shot outside his home on the Acorn housing estate in Toxteth.

He lived in a flat on the estate with his girlfriend. His girlfriend said that she was at home at 11pm on the night when she heard screeching brakes and then the sound of bangs. She said that she then ran outside and saw Hussain Obad sitting in his car and then saw him stagger out and collapse.

When medical help arrived, he was pronounced dead.

His girlfriend said that when she went out she saw two figures, one to her left and one between Hussain Obad's car and another car that it was parked by. She said that when she saw Hussain Obad collapse she ran back into her flat and called the emergency services.

The police arrested eight people in connection with his murder, but no one was charged. They said that they thought that people knew the identity of the gunmen but that no one had come forward.

His post-mortem stated that he died from a gunshot wound to the chest.

He had previously been arrested and released on bail in relation to the shooting dead of another man in 2000. The police said that his murder was linked to criminal activity and was thought to be part of a gangland turf war.

At the time the police said that it was the fifth shooting in three weeks and noted that all the shootings involved men aged between 17 and 21 and that they were using guns to resolve their conflicts as opposed to how people once solved their issues with fists and broken glasses.

Akbal Brar

Age: 21

Sex: male

Date: 3 Feb 2001

Place: Barra Hall Circus, Hayes, West London

Akbal Brar was shot in Park Parade near Barra Hall Circus at 9.15pm on 3 March 2001.

He had been driving a white Ford Fiesta car with a friend when he pulled up in Park Parade and the passenger in the car started speaking with a black man who had been standing near the shops. It was said that another man then approached the car and fired a shot through the driver's side window that hit Akbal Brar.

The man that fired the shot then went off and Akbal Brar and his friend sat in the car for a few moments and then drove home where they called an ambulance.

Akbal Brar was taken to Ealing Hospital where he later died.

Akbal Brar was a trainee mechanic from Southall.

Frank Anthony Holmes

Age: 61

Sex: male

Date: 30 Jan 2001

Place: London

The death of Frank Anthony Holmes was reported as undetected by the Metropolitan Police in a Freedom of Information request.

No further information is known.

Andrew Michael Williams

Age: 30

Sex: male

Date: 29 Jan 2001

Place: Chicagos Nightclub, Peckham

Andrew Michael Williams was shot in the head outside Chicago's nightclub in Peckham.

Andrew Williams and a friend had just left Chicago's nightclub at 4.15am when they became involved in an altercation with some other men in Peckham High Street near the junction with Bellenden Road. Andrew Williams and his friend were then both shot.

Andrew Williams died but his friend, who was taken to hospital in a serious but stable condition, survived.

Isa-Din Shire

Age: 37

Sex: male

Date: 15 Jan 2001

Place: Sutherland Court, Marylands Road, Maida Vale

Isa-Din Shire was found dead in his home. He died from a fractured skull. An open verdict was recorded because it wasn't known if he was killed in self-defence or whether it was homicide or whether his death was accidental.

His body was discovered after a neighbour went into his flat after finding his door open.

Paramedics tried to artificially resuscitate him after they found that he had no pulse and was not breathing. He was declared dead on arrival at St Mary's Hospital.

He was a former Somalian army officer and known locally as the Major.

His inquest heard that he had had a row over money at a nearby flat two hours before he was found during which he had attacked a friend.

His friend said that he had seen Isa-Din Shire walking back from an off licence in the morning and that they had gone back to his house. The man said that Isa-Din Shire had seen them carrying bags and had known that they had drink. He said that when they got back to his house they started a drinking session, however, he said that when Isa-Din Shire asked another man for some money and was refused, Isa-Din Shire had become angry and had taken it out on him and hit him in the face. The man said that he didn't retaliate because the blow had knocked him to the ground and an ambulance was called for him and he was taken to a hospital. The man said that by the time the ambulance arrived Isa-Din Shire had left and gone back to his home which was about 100 yards away.

Police searched the route between Isa-Din Shire's home and his friends, and although they did find some blood, it was determined not to have belonged to Isa-Din Shire.

The pathologist said that Isa-Din Shire had a number of injuries including an injury to the back of his scalp and two areas of bruising to his chest. He also had a fractured skull with a simple linear fracture running across the back of it, as well as bleeding between layers of his brain. The pathologist concluded that his head injury was the cause of death but could not state how the injury had been caused.

The neighbour who found Isa-Din Shire said that he knew him very well and said that he was like a step-son to him. He said that when he found Isa-Din Shire his front door was open and he said that Isa-Din Shire never left his front door open. He said that he thought that it might have been possible that Isa-Din Shire had slipped, but not with his front door open.

Isa-Din Shire had joined the Somalian army when he was 15-years-old and was promoted to the rank of second lieutenant and had come to the UK in 1988 for training at the Sandhurst Military College in Berkshire. However, it was heard that he became injured and quit and that when war broke out in Somalia he claimed political asylum. It was also noted that his wife and two children drowned when a boat they had been fleeing Somalia in capsized.

Isa-Din Shire was also noted for being a heavy drinker.

Anthony Boyle

Age: 58

Sex: male

Date: 4 Jan 2001

Place: West Derby, Liverpool

Anthony Boyle was killed in a street fight.

He died from blunt force trauma to the head. It was thought that he received his injury when his head hit the pavement after being punched.

He was coming home from a Conservative club where he had been drinking at about 9pm on the Friday when it was thought that he had confronted some youths over their behaviour and was punched in the face. The youths were said to include males and females.

A 15-year-old youth was arrested on suspicion of murder but there are no known charges or convictions.

It was thought that he had told a youth off for swinging on a gate, although the police had said they had been unable to confirm that.

He was found lying in a pool of blood and was taken to the Royal Liverpool Teaching Hospital where he was pronounced dead.

Anthony Boyle had been an electrician and labourer and had worked for the Cammell Laird shipbuilder for most of his life.

Printed in Great Britain
by Amazon